Trust Me, Trustee!

A True Story about Family Affairs, Trusts, Alzheimer's, Lawsuits, and The Lord's Grace

Linda Lassiter

Trust Me, Trustee
First edition, published 2016

By Linda Lassiter

Cover design by Bill Asher

Copyright © 2015, Linda Lassiter

ISBN-13: 978-1-942661-14-6

All rights reserved. No part of this book may be reproduced or transmitted in any form or by any means, electronic or mechanical, including photocopying, recording or by any information storage and retrieval system, without written permission from the author, except for the inclusion of brief quotations in a review.

Published by Kitsap Publishing
P.O. Box 1269
Poulsbo, WA 98370
www.KitsapPublishing.com

Printed in the United States of America

TD 20160606

25-10 9 8 7 6 5 4 3 2

Chapter 1
Pre Dementia

"You might be poor, your shoes might be broken, but your mind is a palace."

~ Frank McCourt, *Angela's Ashes*

LEARNED FEAR

From a very early age, respecting Mother was insisted upon. To be so bold to rebel against that training was unthinkable. Dad would wreak havoc on my backside as well as any other place that he might miss aim on. According to Father, his children were never to violate their mother's privacy. That was simply the way it was. She had her rights. And, Mom's rights dare not be offended. With these well-trained eyes, I never remember seeing my mother half-dressed, not even in a slip. I couldn't look.

I wonder how the childhood I knew, one without God, could have indoctrinated such obedience and respect. But, it did. What had trained me, I later realized, was fear. Anxiety, worry, concern, even terror, became the manifestations which would remain within me like a plague; I had been exposed to it as a part of the way I was raised. It would take a Father stronger than my earthly one to remove this type of training. It would take steps, precepts, and commands to change me.

Unlearned Fear

So it was that step by step, line upon line, precept upon precept, His Word began to command and urge me to "Fear Not!" As a part of that command, slowly, there would come an understanding that His blood is sufficient for such deep wounds as these. The idea would take shape in my mind that He had died to bring healing to my life, and all lives, from the hurt fear brings. Like the protection my father had given to my mother, God wanted to protect me. He wanted me to have a new heart—to replace the one previously overwhelmed and burdened--with His love and encase that heart in a spirit of trust--simple trust.

Yet one would wonder how something seemingly simple could be so difficult to attain. Looking back at His work of removing the fear, imposed through years of harsh punishment, could not be seen as anything the slightest bit close to simple. The word simple would, in my mind, have to be replaced with a word that could actually describe what took place--miracle. His deepening work of cutting away at the sin of mistrust would take on more painful and agonizing, ever knee-bending experiences, especially through a disease called dementia—a disease quietly growing within my own mother.

With children and grandchildren of my own, the sin cutting away task began even as I held on to an echoing childhood refrain and allowed it to bounce off the walls of my mind: "Children are to be seen and not heard." This chorus-like catchphrase made it difficult to speak up or take control at times, even though I soon would be forced to do so by the legal document of the trust Father had put together, chided by siblings who wanted their own way, and obliged by that powerful inner voice still demanding respect and obedience—or else. Fear of taking the least bit of a look into Mother's private quarters, or, for goodness sake, offending her in any way kept my adult heart just as guarded as when Father stood over me as a child; for, within those childhood years, there had been no room to explain offenses. That much was clear. There was no say so or even a voice in matters around father's house. What was an appointed trustee, trained to give privacy its rightful place and keep quiet, supposed to do?

Mother would remain, even after Father's death, to be his first priority and protected sweetheart—she would remain to be first in my quest to help her in her confused mental state, in part, because I couldn't let go of my past. The same insecurities and apprehensions, even though I now knew God, continued to dominate my thoughts even as mother forgot a house key, a friend's name, or where she was going. Indicators revealing that something was amiss were instinctively overlooked as if they never happened. Dad would have called that respect. He would have been proud of me.

Respect Your Mother

I would simply dismiss the signs. Perhaps they would go away. What wouldn't go away, though, was the belief that Dad, gone now, had left her unguarded and unprotected, and what she needed was me to watch over her. When my head hit the pillow at night, I could still hear him saying: "Respect your Mother!" When I drove to work, I could hear him repeat: "Respect your Mother!" Disgracing Father's wishes goaded and shoved me to keep on my toes and figure out how I could do something—anything. My mother's dignity was at stake. Even the decision I had made at twenty-four to accept Christ's love and death for me, had reinforced this stand. Hadn't it?

> *"Pure religion and undefiled before God and the Father is this, To visit the fatherless and widows in their affliction, and to keep himself unspotted from the world." (KJV James 1:27)*

To support me in this test of respecting and protecting my widowed mother, at all costs, my husband sold our home, and we moved to Sacramento, California, which houses close to 500,000 people, from Riverton, Wyoming, which is a town of a little more than 8,000, in an effort to be there for Dad's bride. The immensity of the city life that surrounded her had had a far larger effect on us than we could have imagined. We, living in mom's house after years of having our own place, struggled. And we wrestled with job hunting, for we didn't know the folks in this metropolis.

Knowing folks had been a way to secure work where we had lived. After long searches, though, I found a part-time job teaching English at a college while my husband found a sales job putting debit/credit card machines in businesses. He made six hundred dollars that first month; I will never forget it. I made just a little more. After buying gasoline to drive to those jobs, paying mom rent, and buying our food, we began to worry about our situation. Trust God, you say? "He gave us brains didn't He? We should use them."

The Difficulty of Respecting

All the while, God was laying out a plan bigger than our most lofty thoughts or brains could imagine. But, we, blind as we are, didn't see what was happening or realize that He was working. We were busy using our brains—those brains He had given us. While we were busy, Mom's situation and mind was growing more frail. In spite of this, she seemed to sense our dilemma more than hers. Or was it that she sensed hers more than ours? After spending six months in Sacramento, she simply said one day: "I want to do this on my own." How had I, through empathetic eyes, forgotten that she not only was Dad's protected princess, she had always been independent.

At fifteen, when Dad was away during World War II, she lived in an apartment over a bar before she would stoop to living with his folks. Her declaration should not have come as a surprise. But, it did. It caused us to question why God had given us the means to sell out, move out, and try to help out. At that time, in our anger and bitterness, there was no grasping hold of an answer. Answers would have to come later-- much later—when we, through tears, would take the time to look more closely at the spiritual puzzle pieces laid out back then. It all seemed to be nonsensical. What none of us, mom, my husband, or I, sensed was what would soon advance within Mom's aging mind—advance and turn into the unthinkable—so unthinkable that respect could never cover or erase it.

With disappointment guiding us, our decision was to go back to where we came from—Wyoming. My husband drove to our home state with our belongings while I finished my class at the college. We had no idea what was ahead of us. On my drive home, I gave him a call; he sounded terrible. He really could not explain what was going on with him physically. He merely said, "Just come straight home. I need you." When I got there, he was so ill he couldn't even open the door of our son's apartment. Painstakingly, he successfully, at long last, opened it only to reveal the depths of his sickness. I tried to give him water and thought that a bath might relieve some of the pain. Instead, I created greater problems. The water caused more gut pain, and it was impossible to get him out of the bath tub.

In desperation, partly because we had little money, I phoned our church and asked if they could help me get my husband to the hospital. Once two of the elders from our church got to the apartment, though, they insisted that the church pay for an ambulance. They thought there was no way they could get my husband down the stairs, into a car, and on his way. If only he could get to the doctor and be given a quick fix, I thought, he would get better. I knew it; or did I?

After examining him, the physician found that his guts had blown, and he had lain, through all of those three days we were apart, in his own excrement. He was septic. The nurses and doctors did not give him much chance of living.

"Why God? Why?" I asked.

Learn to Trust

God kept silent. His silence and my desperation drove me to His Word begging Him to speak. Very slowly, He would reveal Himself and His love for us. Through His revealing, I would begin to touch on the hem of a realization—just the hem—of what He wanted from me—what He wanted all along—trust—not simple trust—total trust.

> *"Trust in the Lord with all your heart, and lean not on your own understanding; In all your ways acknowledge Him, And He shall direct your paths." (KJV Prov. 3: 5-6)*

> *"... in him will I trust: he is my shield, and the horn of my salvation, my high tower, and my refuge, my savior; thou saves me from violence." (KJV II Sam. 22:3)*

I would earnestly begin to pray while one doctor tried to cut away bad tissue and put a colostomy on my husband's side. Four hours later, I was told, "that it didn't work." I would not cry Why God—not this time. I would, instead, open my Bible looking for answers for the questions filling my heart—how Lord—how do I trust?

> *"The Lord is my strength and my shield; my heart trusted in him, and I am helped: therefore my heart greatly rejoiceth; and with my song will I praise him." (KJV Psalm 28:7)*

God was teaching me to praise Him and to be filled with joy no matter what this world was bringing into life. I was weak—very weak. Once again, His Word revealed just what was needed for that moment. God could be my strength when I was weak and my shield against what I thought was the most difficult trial in all of life; I didn't know more was to come—not yet.

This time, my weakened husband, back on the gurney, is operated on again by a different doctor. It is Christmas. My gift comes once again in a single word--successful. Successful! Hooray! My prayers have been answered. Or, have they? Excitement would be squished and trust as well as my joy and praise would wane with the sound of another single word—"but."

"But, your husband needs to get the poison out of his system--a lot of it. This won't be easy. He has been weakened by the poison and two surgeries. He may not make it," the doctor said.

Bent Knees

Nineteen days, sometimes half conscience, my husband would lay and battle. As the sounds of beeping monitors filled my ears, I began to grasp hold of the idea that God never gives up on us even when our hearts wane and wobble with trust. God never gave up on me or him. Unlike me, whose heart grew weary, He remained strong and sure—steadfast--faithful. Who He is made me want to stay close —and on my knees. I wanted to learn how to trust—fully and totally trust. My impending loss was teaching me that trust means seeking Him, finding Him, and relying on Him—with my undivided attention--not my brains, not my family, not even my husband—just Him.

Slowly, the pieces of the puzzle were coming together. The pieces of my life so far—fear of failure, fear of loss, and now fear of death all fit together. The pieces appeared as thieves robbing me of my purpose. Why God? Not why hadn't You done as I pleased—why hadn't I seen these ugly faces before? Why hadn't I seen that trust comes through grace—the grace of God—grace to bring a husband, half alive, home to a small house? As I began to let go of these three ugly faces—rejection, loss, and death—I began to see that trust frees a person.

Would I let freedom reign as I changed bandages and my mother phoned to say, "I cannot come out to Wyoming at this time of the year. It is just too difficult for me." Or would I again allow bitterness to overtake and control my heart—the one God had been working on? My heart had been softened through the grace God had shown and now through tears—tears for a church that continued to minister to us in the healing days that followed. Like raindrops, they fell at the thought of their love, their giving, and their prayers. My husband and I, who wanted to help others more than to be helped, had only the strength left to be thankful that we were alive and together. We weren't allowed to help our mom, and now we couldn't help ourselves. How strong these Christians were, who gave so much to us during these days of healing. Could we ever be so strong?

God didn't stop working there.

> *"Being confident of this very thing, that he which hath begun a good work in you will perform it until the day of Jesus Christ."* (KJV Phil. 1:6).

TIME AND US

Three years had passed since leaving Sacramento and those dark days of sickness, surgery, and healing. We were confident that He was working even though darkness surrounded us just as it surrounded mother alone without her husband. Something was going on with mom, though, that went beyond the loss of dad. Something different. As she sat in her home night after night, only venturing out to church or Bible Study or, at times, to drive to a store for her food, she was slowing down to a snail's pace—slower and slower.

She was losing touch with others, missing church, losing weight, and losing more of her memory. Dementia happens so gradually. One hardly notices the changes taking place, even when you see the outward signs, the rational mind can hide what is going on, especially when one does not want to admit that there is a problem. When I was forced to look at what was happening, I longed to love on her, but that wouldn't be allowed. I knew that Mom had never really been affectionate. She was a private person and independent even when she had a need.

I justified her actions once again and told myself, "It is just old age. That's all." I even defended her repeated story telling antics. Surely it could not be anything else but age, for she was going on eighty. That's pretty old. What does it matter that she tells the same story three or four times—or more? Even as I tried telling her that she was repeating, she would giggle and go on.

"Did I ever tell you about the time that I rode a horse for miles just to go swimming?"

"Yes, you just told me," I said.

"Did I ever tell you about the time that I rode a horse for miles to go swimming?" she repeated.

"Yes, mom, you just did." I said once more feeling odd at doing so.

How peculiar that she laughed at this.

It was just as strange that one of my sisters, Bridget, the one that now lived with mom, told me about the story telling and the repetition and giggled too. She was the sister born right after me. We had always been close. I was thankful Mom's home could become her refuge after she divorced, lost her job, home, and children. This seemed a good situation--Mom had someone there--my sister had a place to live. As time went along, she too found her refuge to be a house of fallen cards.

There were conversations between us about how Mom was demanding and controlling. I didn't doubt it. Bridget said, "No matter what, I'm not going to give up my weekends away from her." Then there were hints about Mom's car—the new one she had bought on her own after Dad died. "Mom's car is mine after she dies." Why would she claim Mom's car before she had even passed away? I wondered. "Trust me, He said—Trust fully." "Really?" "Trust in the midst of greed?

The repeated stories continued—no they escalated. Though she forgot she had told that story over and over, she never forgot that the shiny new Toyota of hers--ever. She was confused about where she was sometimes—but never about her car. When my sister flew out to see one of her sons, it was agreed Mom would take her to the airport and pick her up later on. All was well in the leaving. Mom was phoned to remind her to pick Bridget up. She had gotten into her car and drove to pick her up, but on the way, she had forgotten why she was in her car or where she was. She was lost. Forty miles past the airport, she recognized where she was and turned around and headed back home. This left my sister waiting at the airport for hours; until at last, she paid a cab to take her home.

Cars and Dementia

The year that my sister moved in to Mom's place, we had driven out. Mom decided she wanted to take all of us to our old homestead, which was an hour's drive away. It wasn't the old place that shocked us. It was the driving. I had never been with a driver who disregarded oncoming traffic, signs, or pedestrians—simply didn't see anything or anybody as she drove. I had never been with a driver who had dementia either. She looked but did not see. We, my husband, I, and Bridget thought we were goners. My husband talked convincingly, and mom let him drive home. Every sane person in that car was thankful.

To think that she drove that car to church, Bible studies, and shops was frightening indeed. One night, after church, she drove home safely enough, at least she made it home, and then she proceeded to lock her keys in the car and lock the garage door behind her so the car would be safe. Locked out of the house and the garage, she thought she could crawl into a window somewhere. After hours of sitting outside, thinking, and trying to wiggle in, she decided to ask the neighbors for help. Still too independent for her own good, she hated asking—hated it. Forced to because she was getting colder and colder sitting outside in the dark, and unable to wiggle in, she finally said the words—help please.

A lock smith opened the door and the car, and mother quickly dashed into her home at mid-night. Every little detail of her actions were causing me to think about what might, in some distant future, have to be done to give her assistance. How in the world, I thought, would I do that without invading her privacy? One thing was for sure, there was no hiding from God's plans; that much I was sure of by now. God, who was still at work on that fearful heart of mine, began to send a strong spirit alerting me of pending trouble to come.

Chapter 2

The Call for Help

"Alzheimer's is the cleverest thief, because she not only steals from you, but she steals the very thing you need to remember what's been stolen."

~ Jarod Kintz

THE PHONE CALL

I couldn't remember how our conversation started as I sat contemplating my sister's comment: "You need to buy a plane ticket and get out here." Reasons behind my decision were mulled over as I sat crammed next to a passenger who took up her seat and part of mine. "Why had I thought this was so urgent? Why had I bought that ticket?"

There had been no earnestness or logic in what Bridget--that silly sister I had played school with as a child--normally talked about on our periodic phone calls. Nothing in one of those previous conversations came across as outrageous, unordinary, or shocking. I heard, instead, gossip and negativity about how life was stressful for her living with Mom. I knew it wasn't easy. It was her cackles this time after each bit and piece of information that caused me to feel the need to buy that plane ticket and come.

Mom had a way of wearing on her four children—each of us with buttons—each fastener to her had a special purpose. The unraveling of those buttoned up nerves of ours began long ago--in childhood. As adults, and grandparents ourselves, we knew she never wanted us to grow up and wouldn't stop trying to use those controls.

She would hold on to old parental expectations so tightly that none of us could get free. Bridget lived with demands, controls, and affronts. Within these dominations, she also lived with a Mom who loved her in her own way. That love would, as always, be dependent upon mood. Bridget's outbursts and embarrassed expressions on the phone revealed more than this moody love of Mom's. It revealed a deep, gloomy, overshadowing change--an out of control moodiness. It was, indeed, a mental roller coaster—a roller coaster with ups and downs–ins and outs—twistings and turnings. Unlike other roller coasters, this one would take us on a ride and expose us to the truth about dementia.

I had been thankful that my sister was living there, if only part-time, because Mom was in her eighties. It took the responsibility—a little bit of it—off my shoulders.

UNEASINESS PUSHES THE FEAR BUTTON

Along with that appreciation, I also sensed that all was not well in the home for either of them. An increasing uneasiness existed within me, a fear, which I held on to no matter how much praying took place—no matter how much I remembered the Lord God had asked me to trust. Mom would talk, when I phoned her, about Dad not being with her anymore with a deep distress in her voice:

"That dirty dog left me. How dare he? You know, he never did grow old. He remained a kid all of his life. It was I who always had to take care of the responsibilities."

There was only silence as I listened and knew she was right.

"Why did he leave me like this?" she at last asked.

She also spoke of death—her own. While listening, God kept urging me to be the caregiver He wanted for those weakened by age:

"Cast me not off in the time of old age; forsake me not when my strength faileth." (Psalm 71:9 KJV).

Once again, I remember my father's words, "Respect your mother."

Death Begins to Stalk

After selling our home and moving out, our earlier efforts, five years prior, had not worked. A sister living there became second best. But second best was not good enough when that great enemy, death, kept stalking closer and closer. It was obvious that efforts to hide from the adversary and take cover behind someone else, namely my sister, who was doing what Father expected of me was not letting me rest. I had been afraid of death all my life. It plagued me like a ghost and brought with it my natural tendency to fear.

I felt his presence growing stronger and coming dangerously close to my heart. When death comes close, it is weaker Christians who become fearful and often allow trust to disappear or fade. The enemy of life has the power to rob even the most seemingly strong. . Mom's age was revealing this truth more with each passing day. He had certainly taken away physical strength as well as mental stability from the mother I used to know. Each week her voice grew weaker—fainter and fainter—almost a whisper. The fear of age and death overtaking her dominated my mind while yet another fear stalked across my thoughts—a fear of where she lived.

Fear of Traffic

Our childhood home was in the country where horses and fields used to fill the spaces around us. Birds had sung so loudly in the trees out back that there were times we could hardly hear each other speak. Hawks, sparrows, crows, doves, eagles, and a vast number of other varieties had come to roust there. We even had a toucan--which came from someone's cage--fly into those trees one time. That solitude and quiet—those piercing and melodious songs--had long since been replaced with another noise bringing with it chaos. The country road outside the old home place had grown into a freeway of sorts. Cars drove by--exceeding the forty-five mile an hour speed limit--sometimes flying down the road at seventy to one hundred plus miles per hour. Just pulling in or out of the driveway could kill you if you weren't careful.

Mother made it clear that she was still driving her car. "No one is going to tell me I can't drive," she said. The image increased my fearful tendency. And, besides the traffic and the road, there were few neighbors around, and because of that independent spirit of hers, those that were around never checked on her. No one was there except for my sister, Bridget—the one who stayed from Monday through Thursday every week. She was alone out there in the country except for an occasional visit from another sister, my baby sister, Susy—the one I had carried on my hip and taught to walk and talk—the one who had overdosed as a teenager and was now a Bi-Polar/Schizophrenic.

All of the factors surrounding my mom's life should have prepared me for that urgent call and the disaster I was about to witness. Instead with hands shaking and the heart pulsating, I was a far cry from prepared. Nothing could prime me for this. The very trust in the One who had stood by me faithfully, as I watched my husband fight for his life, was dwindling. All I knew to do with my God was to beg and plead:

"God, I want things to be normal! Change this quickly. Don't make me go through this. Help me. Please help me. What am I supposed to do?"

With trust pushed aside, the enemy of all faith—fear, and instigator of death--crept into and took over my heart with even greater power. He was taking over my very being at that moment.

Fear of the Unknown

"How can I take control over Mom's life—her happiness, her stuff, her car? How can I when my own life is faltering between believing and doubting? Do You see me? Don't You see that I am not even capable of taking care of her—her needs? How can I step into her private places when I can't even look and feel right about it? How God?" I prayed silently to myself.

I breathed deeply hoping that somehow air itself would strengthen me. It was early summer. My arms filled with goose bumps, and I quivered with a sudden chill as I listened to Bridget's words. All the while, she kept driving away from the airport and toward our old home. Phone calls had been much easier. My logic sought to explain away all that she was saying and step instead into the safety of denial. Surely, here in person, my sister was exaggerating in a hope to get out of some new turmoil she was experiencing. Surely, she was wrong.

My ears pricked up as I heard her words: "Mom was in the driveway when I pulled in from Reno. She was talking in gibberish. None of her words made sense. I didn't know what to do. That is when I told you to get the ticket and get out here." She said. "Can you believe that she was even walking down that busy road of ours? One other thing, she is making eyes at Ronald." She went on.

"What?" I questioned disconcertedly. "Surely, you heard her wrong." I suggested.

"I wish," she answered. "I wish."

What Bridget had just said shocked me somewhat like a time I had driven off of the road and was quickly awakened from slumber by the loud sound of gravel beneath my wheels alerting me that I was driving off the road. What Bridget had said aroused my attention just as the ear splitting sound of gravel under my tires had.

My brother-in-law was twenty years older than my baby sister—the bi-polar sister who needed mental support, and he had abused her for years. Both of my parents, who valued and taught us to respect and obey, had doubted their efforts at backing such a marriage. They had originally hoped Susy could find happiness through marriage. They quickly saw that obedience to this man was out of the question and spoke openly against his antics—to Susy—to all of us. Mom was flirting with this seventy-three year old abuser, smiling, cooing, flipping her eyes, and laughing at his words. Had she forgotten who he was? "How could she forget him after all of the agony he had brought to her life?" I thought.

Forgetting Manners

While Mom flirted, not with words, but with her body language, both sisters and my brother-in-law were walking around in the kitchen eating out of the refrigerator. This wasn't unusual. They did that whenever they felt like it--just opened the door and took what they wanted. That was the way it was. Mom's kitchen was open to them anytime. What had shocked me about Mom's flirting was being outdone by the upsetting —no, disgusting, way in which she ate with them. My father's sweetheart had always been mannerly, especially about how she ate.

"Ladies eat slowly and carefully." She would tell us.

Sometimes it was downright irritating. It even bothered me when she would dab her lips with a napkin and begin to eat again in that same leisurely manner. I felt like saying, "Just eat." But, I knew better. She never got in a hurry about that ritual no matter how hungry she was. Rude table manners in her children had always been unacceptable and would be met with,

"You are not eating tonight. Go to your bedroom."

Not that day. She was shoveling food into her mouth with both hands as if she were a starved animal. To add insult to injury, she was picking at the inside of her nose as if she needed to scrape plaster off of it. The image was more horrible than my wildest imagination could grab hold of.

"Mom," I said. "You have food on your mouth. Here is a napkin."

She responded back to me all right, just not with any words I knew: "Awwek…Awwek…Awwek…DaDaDaDa…MMMMMMM… OOOOOOOOO"

She needed help—or—was it me that needed help? My head was spinning with all the day had brought.

One thing was for certain, there was a need to find some tangible way to care for my elderly mother—the mother who was mumbling nonsensical words. This same mother who was lowering her own standards—the one who felt she was capable of taking care of everything when she couldn't. While I sought solace and understanding, my sister's dark eyes kept searching mine for hope and direction. She didn't know that there was nothing but helplessness inside of me.

My faith faded and weakened as I found myself stuck in a situation I wanted out of. The struggle between feeling caught and doing what God wanted me to do would begin a process of transformation that would change me forever. The quick flight out, and now the sights and sounds I was witnessing, presented to me a heavy weight of responsibility—more responsibility than I had ever carried before.

This would be only the beginning of what would be a four-year-long experience, an experience one should never have, an experience that drove me to my knees sometimes for hours and hours—every hour, every day, and every year. They were the knees of brokenness. These are the kind of knees that God wants us to have. They are the knees that can bend to an Almighty God for direction, love, support, assurance, confidence, hope, and for mental and spiritual healing.

Upon brokenhearted knees, weakened and filled with mistrust, and beneath prayers watered by tears that kept falling and falling every time the body was lowered before Him, the Helper was always there. The more often we, His people, go to this place, the more we can rise up and continue in the battles life brings. Being with Him became my greatest desire after being thrown into this situation. But, I was just beginning to understand what He meant when He asked me to trust.

Dr. Johnson

In July of that awful year, the two of us stressed out girls, Bridget and I, took Mom, in that shiny grey Toyota she had proudly bought on her own, to the local emergency room. We thought that maybe she had suffered a stroke because of the way her face appeared, her speech problems, and the way she carried herself. Upon our arrival, the attendants directed us into a room with hardly enough curtains for privacy and asked that mom put on the green gown with the open back.

If we were not careful, for goodness sake, her butt would show. It was awkward as we tried to help her get dressed, sit her on the bed, and wait, only to have to help her down, take her to the bathroom, then get her up on that bed again and pose her just so. Like the stewards of her privacy that we were taught to be, the two of us kept up an effort at covering and protecting her from anyone's view including our own. It seemed an eternity before the doctor came to examine her—an eternity is a long time to hang on to dignity.

At last, the doctor came and gave us a quick diagnosis, "She will get better."

Apparently, she had been off her medication and had taken dosages improperly for a couple of months. This had triggered the previously silent disease already working inside her. What we were not told that day was that the disease was more than old age—which is what we thought dementia was. As she was being released, I became concerned over her walk—actually, her shuffle. I asked, "Why is she shuffling?"

"She is old, obviously old," the doctor said.

"She wasn't walking like that a month ago. My sister told me she wasn't," I said.

"That is why she shuffles," he said as he folded his records under his white overcoat. "She is old." Then he walked away.

I thought to myself, that there was nothing wrong with being old. That shouldn't be a reason to shuffle.

"Was it?"

I questioned if this was a good reason to explain her gait?

"She is old?"

"Were all doctors caring for the elderly as blunt and rude as this?"

SEEKING ANSWERS

My sister and I hoped that all might return to normal and get better, like he said. Underneath, we had bothersome questions, unanswered questions and lots of them.

"Who would give pills to Mom?"

She had previously refused to let her kids give them to her.

"How could we prevent her playing with and tossing around her medication like dice?"

"Who would stay with her on the weekends?"

We knew it was too dangerous to leave her.

"How could we keep her from driving that shiny car of hers?"

"Who would pay the bills?"

"Should we get her help, or situate her in a place where she could have help?"

Her four children needed to talk. More than talk they needed to trust in God, but they didn't. My brother was on his way from Denver, and soon we would be sitting together, questioning, and answering. We would be doing this as men do this normally--without God. My siblings wanted nothing to do with Him. Worse yet, I knew none of them believed in miracles. I felt that my faith was sitting on a balance beam between two thoughts. Would I be able to accept answers based on feelings and human reasoning alone? I needed more than that and began to pray:

"Lord please be with us. I need You more than ever before. They see me as a fanatic who knows little about being practical. Please let them see You and Your power—not me. Increase my faith."

TO THE BANK

While we waited for our brother to arrive, Bridget kept telling me that she needed money to take care of things like water bills, electric bills, and trash. I had to agree with her. Those things needed to be taken care of. It was decided to put her name on a separate account—the monies would come from Mom's checking account.

In order to accomplish this, we needed to get Mom dressed and ready for a trip to the bank. We couldn't take her with food all over her clothes. We told her to go into her bedroom and put on what we had laid out. Our training had programmed us not to watch or follow her to the bedroom. Surely, she could do this. Wrong!

Soon my sister was calling me, "Come in here and see this."

As I came around the corner, I saw Mom sitting on the bed. Bridget and I looked into each other's eyes, and like little girls, we covered our mouths trying to hold in any possibility of letting out the least little bit of a giggle. We turned our heads so that Mother couldn't see our grins. If I would have known what I was about to see, I may not have come when Bridget called. For, what I saw was funny and, at the same time, dreadful. The sight of seeing Mom like this affected me with the same childhood feelings I had when reprimanded by my father—shame and fear.

I had looked. I had seen. And I had been appalled. How could I be standing here looking at her breasts hanging over only by a strap clipped in the middle? There she sat. She looked as perplexed as a chicken in a dog house. It was as if she knew something was wrong but couldn't figure out what it was. "The cups go the other way around, Mom," I said.

Her expression hardly changed. We waited for her to move or do something—nothing happened. Cautiously, both Bridget and I moved our hands close to her skin and shifted the cups of the bra from back to front. When we were done, there remained to be no expression on Mom's face.

Together in our efforts to secure money for the bills, we took our delirious mom to the bank. She still couldn't write her name, despite the fact that I sat with her and spelled out her four letter name over and over. Mom had told us, growing up, about the straight A's she earned in her school. Like her eating habits and her expectations, she would accept nothing less than perfection—thus perfect grades. She had set the bar high for her children. How then, could we accept that she--so gifted at math, English, and science--could not spell her own name? That truth was just too difficult, frustrating, and embarrassing to face for us. We pretended that, like the doctor had said, it would get better.

When we arrived at the bank with all the legal documents needed to verify that I was the trustee, forms were filled out to transfer five thousand into an account with Mom's name, mine, and my sister's on it. Mother signed with the letter "x." That account stayed open until October. My sister bought food and paid the bills. We hoped that everything would continue as it was before this incident, but deep down we knew better than that—we really did.

Chapter 3
Making a Change

"To care for those who once cared for us is one of the highest honors."

~ Tia Walker

A Home

While I flew home hoping for a refuge and some reprieve, my brother stayed with Mom for three weeks. Bridget came and went as usual. At home with my husband, the days were filled with peace. There was even time to go for a walk and absorb the sunshine. On one particular walk, I noticed, hidden behind the aspen and pine trees, a home for seniors nestled quietly there. It was the loveliest home I'd ever seen. How odd that I had never noticed it before. The thought crossed my mind that God had just put it there—just for me. Regardless of when it had been built, curiosity begged investigation as I stepped past the neatly trimmed bushes, roses, daises, and geraniums, onto the pillared front porch. What richness, I thought.

My eyes followed the pillars as they left their straight lines forming curls much like the fashion and design of the Roman coliseums of old. An elderly couple sat on white, high backed rocking chairs talking. They turned to smile and say hello as I walked past and into the building. Once inside, the thirty foot ceilings further begged for attention. Those high and lofty ceilings held lovely, crystal chandeliers whose jewels glittered and reinforced the idea of royal living. I thought to myself that this is how older people should live.

As I reveled in nostalgic thoughts of the way things used to be for the elderly, a young lady spoke up. "Hello. May I help you?" Before realizing what was happening, she was giving me a tour of the place. She took me through the dining area with napkins adorning crystal glasses and table clothes neatly tied with ribbons on each corner, into the apartments clean and neat with carpeted flooring and stone counters, then on over to the recreation area with activities going on—sewing, puzzles, games, and music. Along with the physical setting, she began to give answers to my many "how in the world could we" questions.

I broke down under the weight of her answers and cried. Relief mixed with my old hidden fear of offending and tears poured out. How much would this cost? How could we find a facility like this and hold on to her specific Medicare provider? As I walked back home, in spite of my questioning mind, I felt somehow better and more hopeful in spite of my tear stained face.

No Returning

Back in California, Mom seemed, at first, to be more docile and childlike in her interactions with Bridget. She followed along and did what she was asked—but only for a while. During these days, I had dreams of staying away for months, maybe even years. That would have been nice. However, I was foolish because dreams, like vapors, often disappear causing a person to have to face reality and truth.

It hadn't even been a month before Mom was growing belligerent—more and more belligerent. Her childlike obedience was replaced with arguing, which brought back her role as the boss. When a Dementia/Alzheimer's patient tries to take control, though, in their unruly mental state, it is difficult for a caregiver not to panic. It was no surprise when Bridget's anxiety filled voice came over the phone lines, mingled with Mom's yelling behind her:

"I am not about to put up with someone else handling my pills. Give them to me. I can do this on my own."

Bridget's screamed:

"Buy a one-way ticket and come. Now!"

This time, there would be no returning—none--until something was done. Anything! Something!

AT THE TABLE

That spring day, three of us, Sam, my brother, who had driven back out, Bridget, and I sat around the table-- the same table we had put our elbows on and gotten into trouble for as we grew up. The sun filtered through the lace curtains in windows behind us. Together, we had a purpose. That purpose was to save our mother's life. We had to come up with some answers, while Mother's granddaughter took her shopping. Susy was not stable emotionally and could not go through the difficult process of decision making around the table. For the three of us, then, there would be no pretending that we weren't on dangerous ground. The option of leaving mom in her home even with my sister there part-time was more than out of the question. It was impossible.

Living and dealing with patients who have Alzheimer's is like learning how to play marbles for the first time. You simply win some and lose some. Like multi-colored marbles in a childhood game, we sought to shoot at the Alzheimer's tentacles that were reaching out and infecting us. We had to rid ourselves of the defiling predicament we had been brought into. Anyone coming close to a person with this disease reacts in ways they never would have expected. The disease's sticky limbs have a way of touching and tearing away at the heart and replacing reason and peace with confusion. This perplexity within caregivers is oddly similar to the confusion that exists within the person diagnosed with the disease. The infected helpers are left in a strange state—the same strange state we were facing around the table that day.

It wasn't surprising that we were confused about where to begin as we sat at that rustic table. No one wanted to be the first to speak up. Each seemed to question whether we should even be taking her out of the place she loved--the one she had lived in for fifty years. This was a special place. The rose's, dad had planted for her and she had loved, bloomed red, yellow, pink, white, and mixed maroons. The Fuji Persimmons filled buckets and buckets for all who wanted them, while the Orange Tree at last was bearing its first fruits. Under such mixed emotions, our thoughts came painfully slow.

It wasn't surprising then, that the process around that table—that day—revealed both doubt and difficulty. Perhaps caring is a disease too—a disease that is fueled by a fear of making wrong decisions especially when those decisions are for the one who cared so much for you. Like the mother of an alcoholic who wants their child to stop drinking but cannot stop providing, caring for Alzheimer's patients causes facilitation. You find yourself answering for them, laughing with their mistakes, and not correcting them. It is tough to make decisions and distance yourself from the role of wanting to show love and respect no matter what.

Dishonoring our Mom ripped and pulled on our hearts. Through the wounds various forms and degrees of tension, regret, shame, guilt, and fear came forth in our efforts to discuss the situation. The childhood fears that had been carefully drilled into us—the buried ones we had built walls around—were surfacing. Through the silence, at last, little questions began to be voiced:

"How much do the senior homes in California cost a month?" Sam asked.

"Seven thousand on the low end, and nine thousand on the high," Bridget answered.

"How many different homes did you call Bridge?" I asked.

"Ten," she replied.

Silence came again. Occasionally, gasps could be heard, then that awful quiet filled the air.

"We cannot afford that," Sam finally said.

At long last, responsibility was beginning to push silence aside—the silence that had been so thick at that table—the same table we had noisily eaten at as children. It was good to hear comments. Soon, words began to pour into the hidden places, over the walls, and under the foundations of the hearts of those who cared—hearts hurt by diseased tentacles.

"How much did the senior home in Wyoming want? Sam asked. Remember, we don't know how long she will live," he continued.

"Twenty-four hundred a month," I answered.

"Perhaps, we could move her there?" he speculated.

"No. The state of Wyoming does not have a Kaiser hospital. That is Mom's insurance provider," I added.

"What about Colorado? I live there, and it is only one hundred and thirty miles from your place," he summed up.

Bridget broke in with, "If she lived there, she would have grandkids that could visit and take her to church. Why don't you find out their costs?"

A Plan

I jotted down as much as I could, wanting to keep our time together organized. The last question called for a phone call to the Colorado Senior home. It was discovered that Colorado charged the same as Wyoming. Unanimously, the decision to take Mom to Colorado was made. Soon we would rent room number two hundred and twenty-two, pay the first and last month's rent, and ask her granddaughter to help us drive Mom out. She agreed. The other part of the plan was for Bridget and I to pack up Mom's essentials—bed, television, microwave, blankets, clothes, dishes, and memory items, and take them out in a U-Haul before she arrived.

For the most part, there were no negatives that day, except for one. That negative had previously been hiding behind a wall. It only came out from hiding when I asked,

"What should we do with Mom's car?"

"It meant so much to her. Let's keep it." Bridget said quickly.

There are times when the love for a material thing can develop into a multi-faceted weapon. It isn't the person that causes this to occur, it is the sin. Sin is as deadly as any other weapon is. It can be a gun loaded with bullets of destruction, or sharpened knives that stab others with the point that lust leaves, or it can simply poison those around with the potion of greed.

To mother, that car held a destructive nature. With it, she could kill herself or, worse yet, someone else. Her mind was simply working one moment and disconnected the next. Driving a car requires attention to detail and focus on what is going on around you. In Mom's vacillating state of mind, she held the potential to be destructive. She was neither focused nor attentive and was as destructive as if she held a gun—pointed and ready to fire.

To both my sisters, that car was also becoming a knife. Its blade was so sharp that at times they used it to cut away any concerns for Mom's needs. Both of them held on to the thought that the car was up for grabs. Nothing but the word lust could describe their desires for it. When each one pleaded their point, it pierced me like knives cutting away any respect I had for them.

"Mother always told me that I could have that car when she died."

Bridget said.

Then, she continued, "My old pick up is getting worn out. I am homeless, remember. "I have no one to take care of me like you do. Don't forget that."

Susy would later phone and plead,

"Mom wanted to take care of me and told me that her car would be mine when she died. My husband wanted me to call and tell you that she said this. I have a mental disease and am on disability. Don't forget that."

All I heard coming through both of them that day was:

"Mine, Mine, Mine."

While each of them envisioned a new car in their possession—that prized possession--I questioned what consideration and right we had over Mom's privacy and property merely because she was incompetent. Surely, her age demanded more respect than this. It would be Sam who would speak up suddenly and settle their cutting pleas.

"Mom will need the money to stay in Cherry Creek Senior Home in Colorado at twenty-five hundred a month. Let's sell it."

Later it was Mom, herself, who would beg over the car.

"It is my car. I have been driving for longer than you have lived. Give me the keys."

Because of insistence, she had been given another opportunity to drive it. Greed has a way of insisting on having its way, and greed won't give up even when it's a poison that can kill just as bullets and knives can. I saw clearly why greed sickens God. And, it sickened me.

"So are the ways of everyone who is greedy of gain; such greed... takes away the lives of its possessors." (Prov. 1:19, AMP)

Only when everyone in that car had the day lights scared out of them did common sense meet truth and greed was squelched. Pulling out from a stop sign without stopping as well as driving across the median was more than her grandchildren could stand. There are times when it takes extreme measures to stand up to that old villain, greed. She had to insist that Mom pull over and stop.

The car that had brought mom so much pride had also brought self-destructive tendencies, lustful desires, and greedy behaviors. All of these come, as I was to vividly witness, from sinful hearts. It was good to see it go, and to have the money to pay the first and last month's rent for Mom's new home—fifty-four hundred dollars plus food, doctor's bills, and the previous bills from the old place.

In order to transfer the Toyota's title, I had to bring to the bank my own ID, my Social Security card, and all of the Trust Documents. I went down to the bank two times and spent about an hour and a half both times. I was so glad the money was put into mom's account and the shiny object of sin gone. God only knew what lie ahead of us financially, and I wanted to give my mother the best that her money could buy. My brother, Sam, had told me that he thought Mom might live as long as her father, who died at ninety-six. He would laugh and say, "If we run out of money, his oldest sister, which was me, would take her in." And, he was right.

Her Toyota would be sold two days after we placed her in her new Colorado senior home. There was no honor in the process of placing Mom in her new home. None! There was, in the place of honor, a cold lead pencil in my hand writing down details. It was a calloused, calculated job—only the facts. Keep writing. Record. Record. Record.

Before taking Mom to her new home and leaving her there, we took her by to see how she would react. To our surprise, she loved it. We were surprised and encouraged as she smiled and said,

"Oh, this place is too beautiful. I bet I could run the show around here easily."

But, when we took her to stay, and she saw her name on the front door of her room, she asked in horror:

"What have you done to me?"

Her words made me feel terrible about leaving her even though my mind knew there were no other choices. When her words mingled with a facial expressions that shouted to me,

"It is about time you come, pick me up, and take me home"

I could have fainted from sorrow.

Her look pierced my soul. She clearly was not happy. I had to convince myself over and over again that all of us, together at last, were doing the right thing. I silently began to confess,

"God. It isn't my entire fault. Is it? Please help me not to feel like an abuser to my very own mother. Please. I hope what I am doing does not appear to be ugly. Forgive me."

Not only did I need to support our choices for her, I had to walk away and leave her in the hands of caregivers I didn't even know.

With the U-Haul contents emptied and Mom securely in her new residence, another document had to be secured stating her condition. One doctor's opinion was not good enough. All of the physical and financial needs for my mother from that moment on were not divided among the siblings. Instead they were placed solely into my hands as per my parents' wishes. I now was the trustee officially. I found myself signing so many papers, hiding my own thoughts about doing so all the while. Uncertainty was shouting "who do you think you are?"

When I should have been sleeping at night, I would get up and pace the floor instead. Again, I heard my father's words, "Children should be seen and not heard."

"What am I doing, I wondered. Was it right for me to be seen by everyone as the trustee, answering everything asked of me, and signing papers that are personal about Mom?"

With Mom in her new place, my sibling and my daughter went back to their homes. It was Susy's job to pick them up. She picked up Bridgett, the one who had ridden in the U-Haul with me. Those returning would be together again--together again without a mother or a grandmother. The sister who had been blessed by mother to have a place to live would stay in the old home and guard over the things until I could come back out, have a garage sale, sell the place, and empty our childhood home completely.

Ugly

We had worked together. Hadn't we? All we had known prior to this event in time was nothing but dysfunctional. We never worked well together. We fought. But, we were working together. Maybe we were friends after all and not enemies. I was the second child born. Big brothers are supposed to help a little sister grow up. Sam thought he was helping. He gave me nicknames like ugly to toughen a girl up. I can never remember a time that he didn't call me that. Even though I told myself that he was jesting, it made me feel inferior and worthless.

"Ugly, come here, he sneered. You are ugly. He taunted me and taunted me. Did you know that? You are!"

I would fight and fight him for calling me that. I tore up his army men. I broke up his ball games. I kicked him under the table. Nothing changed him. Nothing changed me. Nothing broke the power that name calling held over me either. Just like the fear my father and mother imposed, I couldn't work with a brother who hated me. When I became a teenager, my brother shielded his friends from me. He didn't want them to like me, have anything to do with me, or talk to me. I wanted my brother to like me.

One time, when my parents left us alone at night, he called to me from behind the bathroom door. He quickly opened the door and showed me what a man was by exposing himself. I was thirteen. I ran away and hid in the field outside. When my parents returned, I was punished for leaving the house. Still, I wanted him to like me. What happened was never discussed.

I would not betray him. He was a man now—I knew he was. Would a man like me better? No. Both of his wives upheld his hatred. When I came near, they either left or turned their backs on me. I wondered what they were told. I so wanted his approval and love. I so wanted not to be ugly. Did he think that what I did in moving Mom was ugly? I was ever so happy that we were working together. But I couldn't help but wonder and care about what he thought. Regardless of my desires, nothing could break those chains he had woven around my thoughts—thoughts about myself—my ugly self. Until, my Savior reminded me about what He wanted most—trust—complete trust.

Garage Sale

There were financial decisions to make. The cost of her new residence would be expensive. Our resources would have to come from her country home, her car, an annuity, and two CD's. I would purchase another ticket and fly back out to Sacramento to put together a garage sale and clean out mom's home. The sister that lived there had separated Mom's things. Some were too precious to sell like pictures, quilts, crocheted afghans, letters, Bibles, and trinkets. Those were placed in her old bedroom for safe keeping. There were things that Bridget begged for as well—a bedroom set, wall hangings, some blankets and quilts, and a chair.

We thought that since the house was on a busy street, all we needed to do was price and put up signs. The pricing took hours and hours. In the end, the bottom line went over what most wanted to pay. Throughout the two and a half day sale, tags were changed. I kept a detailed list of what was sold so that there would be no questions about what was brought in. I began to think that my siblings might question me.

The sale and the list went on and on until at last we made a little over one thousand dollars—just a thousand—that's it. I felt exhausted, guilty, and fearful—no different with or without Mom's things.

Chapter 4
Living in a New Home

Do not ask me to remember.
Don't try to make me understand.
Let me rest and know you're with me.
Kiss my cheek and hold my hand.
I'm confused beyond your concept.
I am sad and sick and lost.
All I know is that I need you to be
With me at all cost.
Do not lose your patience with me.
Do not scold or curse or cry.
I can't help the way I'm acting.
Can't be different though I try.
Just remember that I need you,
That the best of me is gone.
Please don't fail to stand beside me.
Love me 'til my life is done.

~ Anonymous

NUMBER 202

When Mom first moved into apartment number 202, it was June. She was going to be eighty-one that September. To encourage her, I thought a party would help. Soon, invitations were given to folks living in apartments on the same floor as well as to relatives living in the area. A cake, some balloons, paper products, and ice cream were bought, and a party was taking form. In all, there would be twenty-five partiers eating and having fun. The last day of September was sunny; fall filled the sky with the splendor of yellows, reds, and browns. It was a perfect time to celebrate eighty-one years.

Included in those invited was Nancy. Nancy loved Jesus and wasn't a bit silent about Him. She told everyone about her precious Savior. "I'll soon be with him," she'd say. She had such severe arthritis in her back that it bent her over. To look at you, she had to uncurl. However odd it was to watch her do this, it was worth every effort in the end to see the glow on her face. And, oh that smile. It was a smile that immediately won you over. She would often tap people on the back and say, "Oh, get me out of here." Then she would laugh contagiously. Unlike many of Mom's other neighbors, whose hair was gray, Nancy's hair was a dirty blond. But, it wasn't her hair, her smile, or her face that made her beautiful. It was her spirit.

We, humans, sometimes fail to see the spirit of a person, even a person like Nancy. God never does. 1 Sam 16:7b tells us "the Lord seeth not as man seeth; for man looketh on the outward appearance, but the Lord looketh on the heart." (KJV) In spite of or because of Nancy's sweet spirit, Sam hated it when she sat next to him at the party. His blank stare carried a warning—don't touch. But, his stare never affected Nancy even when his eyes rolled as she began to speak.

"Your mom says that you don't know Jesus as your Savior."

Sam shook his head no, partly in answer and partly in disgust.

"Well, son, you should do something about that. Don't you know how Jesus loves you?"

Sam shook his head no again, harder, hoping it would ward her off.

As if she were deaf to his efforts, she continued with greater enthusiasm.

"You should do something about knowing who Jesus is and what He did to show His love to you. Otherwise, it is a problem--a big one--an eternal one."

It wasn't long after her last sentence that I saw Sam move to a different spot around the table. Nancy just smiled.

Mom's new apartment was soon filled with the love and gifts she had received making it beautiful beyond expectations. There were arched stairways carpeted in Victorian reds and blacks leading up to her door, and a glass elevator that could be used by those who did not want to take the stairs. As the elevator moved upward, the richness of the seating area below was revealed. A grand piano set on one end while luxurious couches could be seen placed here and there. A library, craft room, puzzle table, pool room, beauty salon, and exercise/meeting room were also to be found within the doorways on the lower level. In the background, soft music played.

After arriving on the top floor, Mom's apartment was the first door to the left. It was immaculately clean and would continue to be cleaned once a week by a maid. She had so many television channels, she probably would never be able to watch them all. Her furnishings were arranged just as they had been in her old country home. The same drapes she had at home now decorated her bedroom window, and her cross stitchings hung on the new walls. She had a kitchen complete with a stove and refrigerator, a living room, a bathroom, and a bedroom. I had brought my sewing machine and set it on the floor so she could, if she wanted to, sew. It was perfect for her; I thought.

Two Directions

Or, did I? Perfection or not, there was nothing picture-perfect within my heart, even though her children's plan had worked and accomplished all that was set out to be done that day—at the table—the table we had eaten thousands of dinners on while growing up. Worry about being disrespectful kept plaguing me. My heart was behaving like a teeter totter holding on to fearful thoughts with all of its ups-and-downs while continuing to tell itself that I was doing the best I could. Whenever fear rose to the top of my mind, I tried quickly to stuff it under, especially when Mom would question me:

"Why is my name on this door? Is this what it all comes to?"

With a stoic face, I tried to appease her,

"We love you Mom. This place will help you stay safe. There are lots of people your age here. You can make friends. Remember how much fun you had at your birthday party? I need to go on to my home again, but I'll be back. Bye, Mom. I love you."

I cried on the one-hundred-and-thirty-mile drive home because the answer was yes; you have to stay. Yes. I have to leave you here. Yes. This is your new home. Yes. Yes. Yes. I tried to smile through the tears. And oh Yes, how I questioned God:

"Lord, couldn't it be some other way? I hate this. Do I have to leave her here? Alone? God. She is all alone. Do you see that? Am I doing Your will or mine?"

While I questioned God, I thought about my father. What would he think? Disrespectful! Uncaring! Unloving! Foolish child! Such thoughts brought no comfort. Not on that day in September of 2009, even as I told myself I had no choice but to leave my mother at a senior home. My heart ached for her and for the end of the relationship we used to have in her country home. My hurt could only be silenced by putting on bandages of justification and pseudo acceptances over what had to be. In spite of it all, I kept hearing Mom say:

"I want to go home. I want to go home."

SIGNS OF DEMENTIA

Audry Wuerl, a social worker writes:

"If your mom has dementia, usually it is the "behavioral" issues such as wandering away" [not taking medication properly; and, talking in gibberish]... that precedes the placement. Also, with dementias like Alzheimer's disease, the resident (your mom) may not even remember who the other family members are, the "new" environment is not familiar, and may start asking to be taken home. All of this is especially trying for family members."

Trying? Tiresome! Taxing! Words cannot explain what having a mom with dementia does to the family—especially when all Mother wants is to go home. The stress of living with the sadness, guilt, fear, and concern begins tearing away the insides of a person. My recourse was to turn to God's Word. My siblings didn't believe in God--or His Word—though, I could see, they needed Him desperately.

As I opened the Bible to 2 Corinthians 1:6, it revealed that "[my] hope... [should be] steadfast, knowing, that as...[if I] am a partaker of the sufferings, [so]... shall [I] be also of the consolation." (KJV). His Word was seeking to teach me how He wanted to comfort, console, and carry me—the trustee—through this. There is no trial too big He can't give comfort. I knew that. The problem was I would know and read about these truths--take comfort from them for a short time--and then find myself going back to square one where worry and fear takes over. It is difficult to understand why I would pick things like these back up. But, I did. If I could only learn to fully trust Him instead of giving in to my continual efforts at trying to figure it all out.

Figure it Out

I understood that all my figuring merely brought me back into a viscous cycle. But, I couldn't stop depending on my own mind, even when I knew that the circling would bring me back to an attention span that was all too short. I continued to distort the whole truth about God. The power of God's Word, though I had just read it, would become overshadowed by my own doubt and self-trust pushing truth to the back.

It was vicious. My kind of upbringing had taught me to question and be in control as well as to work hard. After becoming a Christian, I had even heard a preacher say once that we need to "pray like it all depends on God, and work like it all depends on us." That ingrained work ethic sparked self-determination, ingenuity, and self-sufficiency—each spark pushing trust further back.

My self-made, do-it-yourself attitude was how I approached life and my job as trustee. I would instinctively push as hard as I could to make it work. Driving once a week one hundred and thirty miles one way would be a self-determined chore. I employed my brother, Sam, who lived in the same city, to visit her at least twice a week and wrote him a check for one hundred dollars when he needed it from the trust money. He would take Mom to Walmart to buy snacks or a little of this and a little of that. Later, I would ask him to take Mom to her pedicure appointments once a month to help rid her of black, thick nails without causing infection that so easily happens to diabetics. My son and his family, who lived only a couple of blocks from her, picked her up every Sunday for church. It was a work-a-holics great joy to keep it all going, and I was doing it.

Asking and using people, driving, and taking care of the financial needs were just the beginnings of more responsibility to come. For now, the most difficult responsibility was making sure Mom was happy and healthy and that my heart could be at peace about it all.

Mom was offered free meals for breakfast; dining-hall dinners in the evenings were paid for, and her refrigerator was stocked for snacks, lunches, and her favorite oatmeal breakfasts. In spite of our reminding her to eat with the other people living there, getting her to go down and have breakfast or dinners or even to socialize was difficult—pretty close to impossible. She preferred staying in her room and being alone, and we knew this was the worst thing she could do.

Symptoms

People with dementia often tell you that they are eating when their body tells you something completely different. They are losing weight they cannot afford to. The scale at the doctor's office is telling you that this person is shrinking. All that food bought for them and left in their new homes often spoils and goes to waste. One of Mom's helper's reported to us, after she had been living in the senior home seven months, that she had seen her eating rotten tomatoes from the refrigerator. "Mold on them was a half inch thick," she said. From then on out, I made it a point to clean out and throw old food away—old cakes wrapped in napkins, brown orange juice in bottles, molded tomatoes, black onions, and hardened sandwiches.

Since Mom's weight was declining, another visit to a doctor was imperative. The doctor stated that not only was she needing to gain weight "she scored 9 out of 30 on a SLUMS test (Saint Louis University Mental Status)." A SLUMS test measures mental cognizance. Her score told us the disease was worsening. He urged us to try and get her to eat with the other residents as much as possible verifying our own thoughts about this. When I was with her, I would either take her out to eat or eat with her in the dining room. Even when I was with her, she often picked at her food. What touched me most about taking Mom out to eat was how she thanked me. She would say, "You shouldn't spend so much money on me." I was using her money for goodness sake. I tried to tell her that it wasn't my goodness or my money. It was her money, but she never understood.

During these dining times, she liked to tell me, as well, how much she enjoyed eating in her own place. She still liked what she had eaten for years for breakfast. I knew what she ate: oatmeal, a half a slice of English muffin, coffee, and a half of a banana, even if that banana was black. People with dementia seem to live even more habitually than a mentally healthy person does.

Another sad truth about dementia is that your loved ones might be wearing the same clothes every day. The one pair of light blue pants and that plaid shirt of hers were quickly showing signs of spills, soils, and holes. I couldn't convince her to wear anything else. And, the shower was dry each time I checked it. Even when you tell your parent about the need to take a bath or a shower, they might, like my Mom did, tell you, "I have taken a shower. I don't need another one. I have. What is wrong with you? I have." But, you know better.

Cleanliness is not an easy task with an Alzheimer's patient. They often become mad at insistences and questionings. That independent spirit of my Mom's, mixed with her disease, came forth in stubbornness—a stubbornness that would refuse to obey. Other Alzheimer's patients can become violent. Mom never did.

Perhaps her calm nature came forth because she was being taken care of in so many ways, including her medication. Her blood sugars were regularly checked. A nurse came every day to give her the pills properly. And, she loved that nurse. Once, I came in on her and her nurse. Mom smiled and said, "Meet Emily. She's my nurse, and she has the sweetest little baby girl."

Emily had brought her baby in several times to visit Mom. Mom had even held the eighteen month old girl. That had made my mother so happy. Alzheimer's patients often are more connected to babies or animals. There is an overflowing, unusual happiness within the patient when a child is present. The smiles are more intensive than normal. I noticed how my mother would point to other babies when I took her to the doctors, dentists, stores, or restaurants. I could not help but wonder if Alzheimer's patients didn't unknowingly take on more of the heart of God who loves the little children and warned His followers to forbid them not. Or, perhaps they simply mentally returned to a childlike state themselves.

These moments brought a positive view of her apartment life, easing the guilt my heart held on to a little. Knowing that her physical needs were being taken care of and then learning that she was beginning to walk every day to 40s music strengthened me.

Though her eating habits and cleanliness became more and more upsetting, it was encouraging to see that she started to love her place. She even won awards for walking the most miles in a month. When I walked with her a couple of times, it was evident that she was pretty fast. It wasn't as if I had to push to keep up with her, but I was walking at a good pace. She walked on the upper floor of the complex in a circle and often sang along to the tunes that were being played as she walked. Nurses monitored and encouraged her by calling her by name. There was so much normal mixed into dementia. There were times when questions about her condition became perplexing. Was she really so bad off?

There were other times when everything was abnormal, like hallucinations. After about four months in the apartment, Mom began to tell me about seeing my sister in the hallway with a man. She repeated this story several times saying that Bridget had met a man when she was visiting once. The problem with this story was that my sister had never visited her in her new home except when she helped me move furniture in before Mom's arrival. Mom said, "She had that Mexican man with her. He was making eyes at her. I think he loved her. But, she didn't want to have anything to do with him. They just stood there in my hallway."

Then she would point and say, "Right there."

When a person hallucinates, it brings to the listener a sense of unbelief mixed with wonderings and questionings about what the truth is.

"You are kidding? Aren't you? Do you know what you are saying?" I asked.

At some point, smirks and questionings began to cease allowing a quiet, deepening horror to take place. I looked into Mom's eyes and saw that she was serious. I had to turn and see if my sister and a Mexican man she spoke of weren't standing behind me. She really saw, or thought she saw this. She was so convincing that I wondered if my sister had actually come out without me knowing. Loved ones, like me, experiencing stories of hallucination have to remind themselves that the stories come from a deranged mind.

Another concern for Alchemizes patients is that they do not respond well to emergencies. A prime example of this was in my mother's cooking ordeal with her new stove. As a habit, she cooked enough oatmeal for six or seven bowls so she did not have to cook every day.

As the disease grew worse, she didn't pay attention to the fire getting too hot or to the oatmeal boiling over. When this occurred, oats began to burn on the burner one drop at a time. As the drops of oats increased, the flames grew higher and higher. Fire began ascending causing the alarm to go off. When workers hurriedly entered her apartment, Mom was standing there looking at the fire not knowing what to do. They said she had a look of pondering. Something was wrong, but she could not figure out what it was. It never occurred to her that this was an emergency or that she needed to turn the stove off.

THE FOE

All of the feelings that had been trying to form in my mind, feelings that she was safe and secure, began to diminish with each new negative happening or incident. It became more and more difficult to pretend or put on those mental bandages to hide behind. Underneath my pseudo peace, I began to sense a foe or enemy of some sort lurking. Besides mother's growing disabilities and my efforts at keeping her safe, clean, and somewhat happy, I was plagued spiritually. This foe filled me with fear, even though I knew God had commanded me not to fear and to trust. The enemy was following my every move and oppressing me.

Perhaps, these fears came from what my younger sister, Susy, told me: "Bridget is going to sue you when all of this is over. I just wanted you to know this."

From the moment I heard this, it was as if I sensed an inspector watching. I feared the constant examinations more than I trusted God. His presence was making me want to watch my own back. This watchful attitude of mine was especially potent when my brother was near. I began to ask God to cover me with His hand when I prayed. Instead of trusting and feeling His presence, He seemed to be distancing Himself from me.

There was a shuttering inside and a thought of perhaps exaggerating the enemy's power because of my sister's warning. Surely, my little sister was just upset about Mom being taken from her. She had to be making this up. Yet, God's Spirit within me kept urging to pay heed. The urging did not disappear as time went along.

Could God use my self-sufficiency to curtail the enemy? Would He?

At other times, the thought was to try and keep my fear from God as well as my pride. I didn't want Him to think I was proud of all that had been put into place—all that I was keeping in place.

What in the world was wrong with a little pride anyway? Hadn't I been the motivator behind the planning and executing of moving Mom into a safer place? Surely self-sufficiency couldn't trip me up. Could it?

Chapter 5

Handling Money

"If someone isn't what others want them to be, the others become angry. Everyone seems to have a clear idea of how other people should lead their lives, but none about his or her own."

~ **Paulo Coelho**, *The Alchemist*

ME A TRUSTEE?

The Trustee of an "Irrevocable Trust" has sole discretion over Trust assets. (ultratrust.com). As the new Trustee for my parent's funds, I understood their decision included care of what they had carefully set aside. This understanding brought with it a feeling of honor mingled with a large degree of apprehension. It soon became clear that the job of Trustee entailed both financial and physical needs. What was not clear was how to do the job and cover up my own inadequacies.

Perhaps the incompetency grew out of a childhood demanding simple obedience, no questioning, and absolute respect. As the role of Trustee, there would be no one to give guidance or help in the job of "sole discretion over the assets." What there would be was an unforgettable awareness of the poverty and tight finances we had grown up under. It would be the little things like three new dresses a year and one pair of shoes that held up the awareness. These became tangible components in an unwritten law that taught that no matter how many puddles those yearly shoes walked through, how much the soles began to look like they had tongues hanging down, how much they lapped up and held on to small pebbles or mud clots, or how loudly they sounded out in rhythm squeak—squeak—flop—flop the shoes would be worn for an entire year.

Jobs were scarce after World War II causing Dad and Mom to turn to fruit picking just as my grandparents had done after moving to California during the Dust Bowl. We children would be picked up during wee hours of early mornings and placed in the back seat of our 1949 Buick Sedan. Then we would sleep as Dad drove to the fields. As early as six, working alongside Mom and Dad became normal even though at times the cold would be overwhelming.

All a child could think of was crawling back into the old Sedan and going back to sleep except that sometimes there were the darkened silhouettes of knurly branches that would cause childish imaginations to run wild and dismiss sleep all together. No matter what the fears or wants were, though, our family's livelihood depended upon how many crates were filled. Frugality, financial stability, and hard work became a sort of second nature as we grew.

After marriage, those patterns became just as much a part of life as those childhood lessons had been. My husband had chosen to enter the ministry saying that, "Serving God would be a much more fruitful life" when all I really wanted to do was to crawl back into a secure place, cover my head, and stay away from anything knurly. Human souls became just as important to our well-being as peaches, plums, pears, or cherries had been in my childhood. Not surprisingly, most of our married lives we often lived from hand to mouth. We never really had much.

SELLING THE OLD PLACE

The demand for care of Mom's finances never let me rest. To imagine Mom leaving what she had in my care was often unthinkable. Each financial decision was like a hurdle that seemed impossible to jump over.

After the garage and car sale money was deposited into the trust, and Mom's new home with all of its costs were paid, Bridget and I walked together across the busy highway towards a quieter, country road. Small Shetlands with black and white patches, solid browns, or all black horses ran alongside the fences as we walked. They begged to be petted, given a bunch of grass from the other side of the fence, or one of those carrots humans often carried in pockets. Hawks circled the fields for mice and screeched, while the sunset filled the sky with a brilliant orange. It was there, as gentle breezes touched our faces that I spoke to my best friend, my sister, over how to sell Mom's old place.

"At twenty-seven hundred a month just for Mom's rent in the senior home, the money will drain away quickly," I told her. "We could settle for the low appraisal amount, deposit that money, and pray it lasts for Mom's life span, or we could sell it on a contract for deed and keep the interest pouring in for years to come. That interest would allow us to bring in more than the appraised value." I said.

"How do we go about selling on a contract?" Bridget asked.

"I will need to seek out a title company that can put together a legal contract." I answered.

The option of contract for deed became more and more appealing to both of us as we continued to walk and contemplate.

Another consideration was to keep the place in the family.

"None of my children want it. I have already asked them," Bridget said.

"What about Sam? Do you think his kids might want it?" I questioned.

She replied, "Since he moved to Colorado to be near his daughter, his son is going to move there too. I don't believe either of them would want it. And, Susy never had children." There was a long pause, then she asked, "What about your kids?"

"All of my children live in different states, that is, except for one, my daughter. None of them except her would be even slightly interested," I answered.

My daughter had worked and lived in the same city that her grandmother had for over twenty years. She held a good job and had rented all of those years. The considerations for who bought the place did not matter as much as the consideration for Bridget. She had been homeless prior to living with Mom. Unless she could park on the old place after we sold it, in a trailer or mobile home, or even stay inside the house, she would be homeless once again. Neither of us wanted that to happen. The conclusion that we should offer the house to my daughter on a contract for deed became an answer.

Gut Feelings

In spite of the positives, my guts reacted with pain. The idea of selling to my daughter stimulated a lack of trust and exonerated, instead, that awful fear within me. It became unsettling. What if my siblings used that against me? Though the greater consideration had been given to Bridget's needs, there was something in her eyes that appeared to be devious. Seeking to rid the paranoia, I dismissed the appearance, telling myself we were best friends, sisters.

All of my efforts at covering the fears couldn't dismiss what God's Word kept telling me, "...believe not every spirit, but try the spirits whether they are of God...." (I John 4:1, KJV). As a Trustee, one simply needs to see sin as God sees it. I struggled in doing this by pretending my siblings loved me too much. From that day on, however, Bridget's actions and interactions became more conniving and suspicious. Questions like, "What if you make a mistake?" began to permeate our talks. The whole idea of selling Mom's home to my daughter began to increase the weight of the job. This honorable job kept getting heavier and heavier with each decision.

At first, I had kept careful records of transactions because of concerns over scrutiny and a brother's hatred. But, as time went on and financial transactions increased, I began to slip up on those duties relying on larger contracts and bank account records instead of daily penciling. "It isn't necessary," I told myself.

Besides, Sam seemingly supported my thoughts by saying, "Don't bother sending those monthly accounts to me." And asked, "What am I supposed to do with them?," Thus, I slipped further away from diligent record keeping. It was just easier but maybe not an intelligent decision.

It was ignorant of me to listen, believe, and continue to seek my brother's acceptance. It was also ignorant of me to slack on the record keeping. At that point, it seemed ignorant for me to be the Trustee. Actually, I felt just plain ignorant. Me the trustee! How could it be? After all, who was I?

It would be that work-alcoholic attitude that would drive me. Onward I went. Just do the job—just get it done even if you don't do everything just right! Talking to various institutional representatives, keeping up with bills, making and keeping appointments, driving back and forth, all left little time for my own home, job, and husband. It was driving me crazy. Besides the mental stress and spiritual battle, being a trustee takes time away from whatever life a person used to have. The entire honor once felt disappears sometimes before it is even digested.

Of course, I went to church during these days of stress. One of those times, the preacher reminded people that hurrying and getting things done is not what God wants of us. Instead, he said, He wants us to wait on Him and listen for His still small voice. I wondered how one did that. Like a bird caught in a thicket, I struggled to keep my spirit well and focused on what I believed God wanted of me At times, my nature, not God, drove the pursuits and choices made. "Just do something. Just get the job done." I thought. That type of thinking, I knew, was not of God. Work ethics, fears, and childhood examples drive us all from fully listening and trusting. If only I had sought to walk in His wise bestowment. Instead, often choices made in haste opens our hearts to do the foe's will. I Peter 5:8 tells us to "Be sober, be vigilant; because your adversary the devil, as a roaring lion, walketh about, seeking whom he may devour: (KJV).

The documents for the contract for deed on Mom's old place had been sent by the Title Company to my home, signed, and returned all in one day. There wasn't a lot of listening or praying on my part. Instead, my fearful side quickly asked God to bless the effort, and then I proceeded onward. There was little time to trust and listen for His guidance.

This self-made, frugal, work alcoholic attitude drives a person in the wrong direction quickly. I was phoning and emailing at least three times a week to a title company in California and forcing it to happen. "Good morning. This is the Trustee for the California property. I am calling to check on the proceedings involved in the final contract for deed." I said.

"Laura is working on that, as you know. She will phone you when it is complete."

"Thanks, I said, "but I will be checking regularly anyway."

"It would be better if you didn't."

"This is important to me," I said. "I will phone back." And, I hung up.

All of my insistence was my way of making things happen, and, if that didn't work, I would call on God. This is what determined folks do. Apart from wanting to care for Bridget, part of my urgency to get this done was because she still lived in the house while the trust paid for her expenses.

When prior to the completion of the legal contract, my daughter wanted to rent the old homestead, pay for the electricity, trash, and gas, a decision to allow this was made. Just six months after mom was taken out of her longtime home my daughter began to rent the place for one thousand a month and pay for the expenses. That extra money began to quiet my soul and ward off the stalker, at least for a while, and I could call it God's will.

Finalizing Paperwork

After two months, the sale of Mom's old place was finalized, papers for a contract signed, my sister remained on the place, and my daughter was the new owner. Now even the taxes would no longer be the responsibility of the trust. An escrow account was set up for the payments to be recorded and accounted for. The interest earned on the deed of trust was seven percent. It was wonderful to have it settled; at least, I thought it was settled. All the while, the feelings of a foe stalking close at my heels remained.

With each decision and transaction, there was an additional spiritual weight. Trust in God was becoming more unsteady and that unwavering fear was growing. Each time money was spent to help Mom out or something was sold to restock the account, fear walked closer like a shadow of doubt upon my heels. The threat Susy had told me about made the apprehensions allow the Foe to tell me I was a sneak, a thief, or a fraud even though God reminded me daily that I was His own.

There had been several times of reaching out to my brother for help or advise. He repeatedly told me, "You know I was never good with money. Right? I almost starved to death when my first wife and I were in college. So, don't ask me. Just do what you think is best. Besides, if all else fails, Mom will go to live with you anyway." His statements caused me to rely solely on my awareness of making financial decisions that would sustain life and keep up with the demands Alzheimer's brought.

At the same time, I was selling Mom's old place, Bridgett wanted more of Mom's things. She would argue with statements like, "I've been sleeping on that bed for two years now. I really think of it as mine. I think Mom would want me to have it. And, that picture over the mantle reminded Mom of me. She also would want me to have that. The chest of drawers in the other bedroom is perfect for my daughter, and since your daughter is getting the house, you should let me have that too." Taunting my moves and looking for fault alerted my fears to run away from the requests by just giving in to her wishes.

There were pillows and chairs, and tools that she also kept because she had "earned" them she said. As far as advice, she really just wanted me to do what I felt was best except when it came to things she felt ownership of. "I want my freedom and do not want to be tied down with Mom's needs anymore. It is your turn." She, this sister I loved, bluntly stated.

What was left after the sale was an annuity and a couple of CDs. That money would deplete quickly as Mom's needs increased. This brought me back to the table of decision. I would pray.

Buying a Three-Plex

I had prayed. It wasn't that I decided on the purchase alone or trusted my Lord completely, but I had prayed. I spoke to my siblings as well only to uncover the same answer, "Do whatever you want." It would be my decision, again—my management of funds—or mismanagement. I made the choice to look for a rental unit that I might invest the annuity money into. Not only would the monthly income increase and cover the costs of the senior home, but we still would have the unit to sell after mom passed away. Call it the Lord's leading or simple blessings. I found a three-plex unit near my home in Cheyenne, Wyoming, bought it, under the approval of my siblings, and went to work renting the units out.

I would physically care for the three-story unit, collect the rent monies, and re-rent flats when necessary. The cost of the three-plex was $126,000, which came from cashing in the annuity. Its three units brought in eighteen hundred twenty-five a month. Combined with Mom's Social Security, we would be able to cover the expenses and save some for her future. We estimated that Mom might live to be ninety since her father had. There were also two CD's that expired during the early days of Mom's disease. That money was also deposited.

My cousin had told me that it didn't matter in the end how much money you had when Alzheimer's patients were placed in a nursing home. Those paid for by the state and those that were paid for privately got the same care. This information stirred the work ethic within me even more because worry was what I did better than trust.

Spending on Mom

Besides the greater expenses for housing, medical, and daily expenses, Mom got her hair done at least twice a month. Being able to provide for her in this way was a delight. Like most Alzheimer's patients, she was not showering, and her hair became matted, flaky, and dirty quickly. In fact, the beautician asked me why it was in such disarray. She was still a beautiful woman, and my father would have wanted her to look her best. The money was earned and put aside, I knew, for his special bride first. There was no question about that. Taking her shopping brought another concern to the surface—going to the bathroom and the lack of control. We were in WalMart when I forgot to ask her if she needed to go. It was too late. She did not appear disturbed about it – I was though. Quickly clothes were bought, paid for, and put on. This is yet another challenge to the disease – embarrassing the caregiver.

Her nails were done every two weeks as well partly because of her diabetes. Cracking, breaking, or peeling nails could cause infection. It was just safer to have them done. No one would cut them at the senior home because of liability, and Mom certainly could not care for them herself. When she was at the nail salon and sitting in front of the attendant, she would flip her hand up in the air and curve it down and say, "Aren't I just something? So beautiful!" I laughed and told her that she certainly was.

Such small expenses made so much difference in her life. Going out to eat or shopping at Good Will was other special treats for Mom. Whenever I made a trip down, going out to eat for a Subway sandwich was her favorite place. She always ordered the same thing: a cold cut sandwich. Mom had eaten baloney for so long it was just natural for her children to serve it. When we were picking in the fruit fields, she would pack us all a baloney sandwich and say "yum" when we sat against a tree to eat them. If we had no mayonnaise, it did not matter. Baloney was enough to make anything good she would say.

There were other sandwiches that she loved too like bean, cow tongue, or pickled pigs feet wrapped in bread, but she could never get us to eat those or serve them to her when she visited. When I took her out to eat, she would smile so sincerely that it blessed me. A person with Alzheimer's recognizes their own likes and dislikes. They just cannot always voice them. Be on the lookout for the smile, though. For, it might just be the smile that tells you they are pleased and happy.

Thanksgiving

With the changing of the leaf colors, Thanksgiving came. For her first Thanksgiving in the senior home, one of her grandsons, living in the area, invited her and as many other grandchildren that could come over. Some came from as far away as South Dakota to be with grandma that day. She was happier than I had seen her for a long while. Alzheimer's patients want to be included in family events too. Love is a powerful healer.

She especially took up with Patricia, a twenty-year old girl from Africa, who was living with our Sioux Falls, South Dakota son. It was difficult to understand the attraction the two had for one another but very evident. She stayed by her side for most of the day. When we played games that night, that petite, African girl helped mom with the answers, just as she would have any failing older person in her own country. "Mom," she said, "Here is where it goes. You can do it, Mom." Here, let me help." Then they would hug and look into one another's eyes like old friends.

Christmas

My brother, Sam, had her over to his home for Christmas, and I was given some time off though I worried how she would cope. I had put up a tree with lights in her apartment, and the Senior home was filled with choirs, bands, and festivities almost every day of December. The people at the home were falling in love with her just as I had prayed they would. She, too, was falling in love with them. We knew that because she was spending less time alone in her room and more and more time with them. There were times I would phone and she would not answer. That was a good sign.

DENTAL NEEDS

There were dental needs arising at this time too. Bridget had worked for a dentist for years, so she would know what insurance we might purchase for Mom. Upon her advice, I purchased dental insurance. Soon after the purchase, I took Mom in for a cleaning. It was at that visit, the dentist called me in to see Mom's back molar. There it was hanging sideways. It was so close to the back of her mouth that it could have fallen out and down her throat at any time. When the dentist wanted to take it out, however, Mother said, "It will be fine. Just leave it be."

"Mom," I said after being called in, "it is going to fall out and chock you." She did not respond which is typical of people with her disease. Sometimes, they just cannot think clearly enough to respond in any way.

Turning to the dentist, I told him to remove it. No pain medicine was necessary. After taking her back to the apartment, removing the gauge, and going down to eat in the dining area, it appeared as if nothing had happened. Besides taking her to the normal and sometimes necessary places, I was able to take her on an outing.

The senior home offered a variety of trips, but Mom never went on any. People in her condition do not want to step out of the familiar. It would be a great pleasure to drive down and go on a bus ride with her. This particular trip was to a beautiful part of Colorado mountains. Mom got on the bus after me. I was able to see her enter the bus like a cheer leader greeting and smiling at all the other passengers sitting in the rows before me. She was all smiles. She was becoming a part of the people, and they were becoming her family. And, I was able to hear a story about my grandfather that I hadn't known of. She told me, "He had wanted to buy property in this valley," she said. "Grandmother would not let him leave their Oklahoma ranch. Isn't it beautiful?"

"Yes, it certainly is." I said feeling as if I had had a mother/daughter moment. It was a special time.

Chapter 6

Breaking a Hip and Rehabilitation

"He heals the brokenhearted and binds up their wounds."

The Phone Rang

"Don't be alarmed. Your Mom has fallen, and we have called an ambulance to take her to the hospital to be examined. She just needs to be checked. Don't worry. Can you or your brother go to Swedish Hospital?" Juanita, the social worker, asked.

After a phone call to my brother, he finalized our conversation by sarcastically saying, "This is all we need." Then, he hung up and was on his way to the hospital.

A hip out of sorts changed everything for the Biblical Jacob when he wrestled with that angel of old, until a heavenly being touched the sinew of his hip. After that, everything in Jacob's life took a new direction. Mom's hip was broken, and like Jacob, everything in her life was about to change.

The operation required placing rods down her leg then connecting them to a rotating ball where once her hip had been. Only three small incisions accomplished this. Modern medicine almost appeared to be as miraculous as the touch of an angel except for one thing: doctors are flawed beings; God's angels aren't. After the operation, she woke up and squinted saying to Sam, "The sun is so bright. What a hot day this is going to be."

"No, Mom. That is not the sun." He told her. "Those are the lights. See them in the ceiling?"

She smiled up at him and told him frankly, " I know the sun when I see it."

We never really knew which came first. Either the hip broke and she fell, or she fell and it broke. We did find out about some of the details surrounding the fall though through a most unlikely source. Ed, another resident at the Senior Home, had been standing close to her when she started to fall. He told us the story.

"I saw her falling and reached out to catch her...the poor thing. I missed her by only an inch which left me standing there watching. She writhed in pain on the floor of the lobby where we had been visiting just moments before. After the ambulance came and picked her up, the worker's became angry at me. They said to me,

"Never try that again Ed. You are too old and frail to help a falling patient."

"I told them that age has nothing to do with trying to help someone else. She was so helpless and frail. I just feel terrible about it. I hope she will be okay and come back. I really hope so." He shook his head, then looked up at us and said, "And, by the way, I would try to catch her again if I saw her falling. Those workers don't frighten me."

REHABILITATION

After the surgery and her time in the hospital, she could not walk. We were told she needed rehabilitation. Upon doctor's orders, she was to be placed in a nursing home for the prescribed rehabilitation. My brother had been forced to choose between two homes. He chose one, knowing nothing about it. Sam told me later that it was like going, "inne meene miine moo. I choose that one."

THE NURSING HOME

As soon as it was dawn, I drove to her rehabilitation home wondering what this doctor's recommendation would be like. It wouldn't be long before I would find out. After entering the building through two sets of doors, a single desk appeared. There was a woman sitting behind it. She looked to be very busy answering phones and shuffling papers because she hardly had enough time to notice my presence, that is, until I cleared my throat.

"May I help you," she routinely asked.

"I am looking for my mother," and I gave her Mom's name.

"The residents are eating currently, so she should be in the cafeteria." She said pointing down a long hall. Walking in that direction, the furnishings appeared homelike yet professional. Newly designed maroon, black, and white carpet lay on the floor, while high back chairs made from dark cherry wood sat around a fireplace. The look changed after entering another set of double doors. There, the floors were made of a gray tile while the walls complimented the grey with a dull light blue. A sour smell permeated the air while groans and shouts filled my ears to overflowing. Why are they yelling? What are they saying? I wondered.

Continuing down the hall and coming to a swinging door labeled dining room, there was an elderly woman sitting slumped over, her head touching the tray of food in front of her. Another arthritic patient struggled to get his distorted hands around a spoon and carry food upwards towards his mouth. It was then that movement on the right side towards the back caused me to glance in that direction. There sat Mom all alone, in a wheel chair, staring at a bowl of oatmeal and a piece of toast.

"Oh my God, forgive me." I prayed. "This is a terrible place for her, especially after surgery. Does she feel forsaken?" I knew she must.

Mom's face was pale. Splotches of gray could not hide what must have been going on within her broken body. Her hair had not been brushed. I wondered for how long. Could it have been since before the operation three days ago? The back of her hair lay flattened while front hairs stuck up in different directions. She was dressed in her blue pants and stripped blouse. It was still unwashed, stained, and in disarray. As I walked closer, she saw me and spoke up. "I never knew it would come to this."

Her weakened appearance combined with the sights and sounds were frightening. I didn't know how to answer her. As I wheeled Mom away from the dining area and down the hall an odd feeling consumed me. It was a desire to somehow make it all better. Once we made it to her room, I gazed about. It revealed a soft green, hospital look, from floor to ceiling. There were two drawers for clothing built in to the left wall and a mirror. There was a curtain that could be pulled around her bed for privacy, if one was physically able. How could Mom possibly pull it, though, since the rod for pulling was too high for her to reach, and she couldn't stand? There was no call button or phone either. The bathroom was opposite her bed and too narrow for a wheelchair, which made me wonder how she might ever use it without help. She could have no money, credit cards, or jewelry in her possession we were told either. Looking down, her feet appeared swollen twice their size. I wondered what was being done.

The Care

A CNA came in disturbing the contemplation.

"I need to go to the bathroom," Mom said when she saw her as if she knew this was her chance.

At once, the CNA began helping her up from the wheelchair and holding her so that she could walk somewhat clumsily to the toilet. The helper had recently come from the Philippines and spoke broken English. I watched as she pulled down on Mom's pants, sat her down, and wiped her when finished. Never had I seen my mother being treated so roughly. It was as if this toileting needed to be done quickly so that she might go on to the next patient. No concern seemed to be present for going slowly and carefully or to giving consideration to age. I shook inside feeling like a child again who couldn't look.

Settling my mother back down into her chair, I went to the nurse's station and asked, "Why is there no phone in my mom's room?"

"It isn't necessary." Came a reply.

"Really? I believe a phone is necessary for us to communicate with her while she is here. And what would happen if she needed help immediately?"

"Mam, it simply is not necessary for these kinds of patients."

"These kinds of patients! What do you mean?," I asked.

"We do not have time to talk to you. You will need to go to the front desk, not the nurse's station," she replied.

"Before I do, may I inquire why my mother is being fed food that is not appropriate for type 2 diabetics? I saw that her oatmeal was sugared and her toast jellied."

The nurse answered, "You will need to speak to the cafeteria. We have nothing to do with a patient's food."

"Aren't records kept on patients by professionals to track their dietary needs as well as their rehab needs? I believe they are called patient plans." I said.

"Mam let me repeat myself. I don't have time to speak to you right now." She answered then turned away.

It was at that moment that my brother was coming down the hallway. We had an appointment with the intake officer. Forms needed to be filled out. The negative sights, sounds, smells, and touches left empty, hopeless sensations for both of us; yet, we knew we had no choice but to keep the doctor's orders. Besides, Mom's insurance company would not allow moving her once she was admitted. So, we signed.

After signing, we stepped into the hallway together. It was there that a nurse spoke to us. "Do not disturb the nurse's station again; we cannot give out any information."

"Really?," I said. "I am her trustee."

"I'm sorry. We cannot talk to you," she emphasized.

Feeling even more trapped, it was good to be driving away from there. It was while driving, that I received a call from the director of admissions.

"Do you have a moment," she asked.

"Absolutely," I replied.

"The nurses you spoke to earlier today were new and did not know that they should be giving information to trustees. I have explained to them that they need to give you the information you need. I apologize," she said.

"Thank you. I have serious concerns about my mother being there as well as her care. Her diet needs to be cared for more carefully, and I noticed that her feet are swelling. Is anything being done about that? Another concern revolves around the fact that her loved ones cannot call or speak to her. She has no phone in her room." I said.

"Oh, we will do all we can to bring her to a phone." She answered.

"That will help. But, why are there no phones?" I asked receiving no direct answer.

"Oh, one other thing," the head nurse said. "Can you come down and go with your mother to her post operation appointment. We don't have enough staff that day to go with her. And, she is not allowed to go alone."

"Sure." I said writing down the information needed for the appointment. I knew a van would take us.

I sat, that day, in a seat against the wall talking to Mom as we went, pointing out the hospital where my granddaughter was born, the beauty of the trees and flowers, the mountains, and the blue sky, all the while working at keeping feelings of nervousness away from Mom.

After arriving and checking in, we were taken into a room where the doctor would see us. There was a computer opened on the desk that revealed an x-ray. When the doctor came in, he asked what my mother's name was then looked at the computer. "She should be up and walking in a week or so. Everything looks fine." He said, then walked out. His time with us was less than five minutes. Mom and I simply stared ahead, until Mom broke the silence by asking, "How does he know I'll be okay." I turned to look more closely at the x-ray which revealed the date Mom was operated on.

I asked a nurse when the x-ray was taken and she replied, "The day of her surgery." I had been correct. The doctor was not looking at her current condition but at her condition after surgery only.

Oh how we treat our elderly, I thought. Mom was right. How did the doctor know she would be alright? The truth was that he didn't.

Each day Mom was in the nursing home, we all grew more disturbed, partly because each time one of us phoned, we were told it wasn't possible for us to speak to her. They simply remained to be too busy.

Because of the lack of communication, it was important that a trip be made every day. On one of those trips, a hair appointment had been made at a beauty parlor connected to the home for Mom. At last, her hair would be clean and neat. It was while Mom's hair was being washed, that the beautician began to talk in confidence. "Sometimes the care the residents receive here isn't the best." She said.

"I noticed that." I said in response.

"Actually, I am not supposed to talk about their care, but I just want to warn you to watch while she is here."

"Thanks" I said as I gulped down my own fears and mingled them together with this new information.

Not only did Mom get her hair done that day, she also had a physical therapy appointment. As the therapist helped her onto a low bed where her legs could be lifted and bent, I noticed the incision by her hip appeared too pink. "Her incision looks like it is infected," I said to the physical therapist.

"Oh that is nothing. It is just a little pink from the surgery. There is nothing to worry about." she said.

"Oh." I said still wondering.

After her exercise was finished, the therapist and I helped Mother up from the low table she was on and got her into a walker and standing upright. She was able to walk for a short distance which was about twenty feet. It was exciting to see her trying, and I told her, "The sooner you can walk; the sooner I can get you out of here."

Mom just smiled and shook her head.

The next day, it was the mental therapist's time to visit. She had a series of questions, and Mom answered them completely and rightfully. It was as impressive as her efforts to walk were. She retained so much past information. It surprised me to hear her spit out that information. The therapist said, "She is the highest scoring patient I have in this nursing home right now."

"Thank you Lord." I prayed quietly to myself as I drove away.

And then my phone rang again. "Your Mom has an infection around her incision and needs antibiotics. You must also know that because of the infection, she could easily decline physically," she said.

The weather was good and the roads clear that day. I had left after the therapist's tests were done and was driving towards home when the call came. I turned around. After arriving, I quickly entered the building only to witness severity. Her bed was raised. The nursing home doctor and three nurses stood beside her inserting tubes and checking them. Her fever was high, and she was unconscious. "Mom had always been strong, I told myself. She is a fighter; she will make it." But, was she strong enough to endure a nursing home, its lack of personal care, its irresponsiveness to questions about her condition, and now a full-blown infection? I thought.

All of her children were becoming more and more upset, but all of us felt trapped into leaving her there until she was healed.

We were trapped not only because the nurses wouldn't speak to any of us, but the resident doctor, who administered her medications, refused to speak as well. I went home praying she would win this battle.

In three days, Mom was getting up and the infection was all but gone. God was being so good to her and to us, that is, until my next visit. As I entered the home, this time Mom sat in a wheelchair with her head hanging down to her waist. "Mom," I said.

She looked up and smiled a smile that was as unsteady as any drunks would have been. I turned to the nurse's station with more questions. "What have you been giving her and how much? I asked then expounded further.

"When my mom first came in, she ranked the top patient mentally. This is what the therapist told me anyway. One week later, the mental therapist tells me to look and see what you have done to her. What is going on? I told them. Mom's head hangs down, and most of the time, her eyes won't open, even when I am talking to her. Why did her mental therapist tell me the drugs created a person who cannot stay awake long enough to think? The bottom line is for you to tell me how many Percocets you are giving her?"

"Six mam, six" she answered.

"A day?," I asked.

"Yes. Of course," she said. "She has been very sick."

"But, six a day is too much. She can't even remember who certain family members are anymore," I said.

It was true. She could no longer identify her loved ones. Her mind was completely blank after being in the nursing home for two weeks.

"Mom, I said, that is Patty Carol. You remember, don't you? You kept her with you and helped raise her. Don't you remember?" I asked.

Half asleep, she raised her head only to let it fall again. Her physical state as well as her mental state was deteriorating fast. It was time for me to be looking for another place. It was urgent.

After surviving the infection and overdoses, she soon developed bed sores on the heels of her feet and on her butt. No excuses for bed sores could be given, except for one—neglect-- especially on the heels of her feet. With each mistreatment, that old self-determined will of mine kicked into a higher gear. I would force change. "Get her out of here no matter what," I told myself. "If you don't, she will die here—sooner than expected." I had to. I had to because after only three weeks she sat with her eyes glazed over, in a wheelchair, helpless, hurting, and the bed sores weren't getting any better.

Chapter 7
The Best New Home

"Earth has no sorrow that Heaven cannot heal."
~ **Thomas Moore**

REJECTION

No one seemed to want a patient in Mom's condition. It had taken hours of telephoning. I begged and pleaded to no avail. The senior home where she had been living wanted to help, but needed to evaluate her. After doing so, the phone rang with bad news. They couldn't possibly take her, but they did give me references and suggestions. More phone calls began to take place. The answers were that they were either full or couldn't conceivably help either.

The urgency pressed me in so that I couldn't let discouragement deter the need to find someone somehow. Night after night, day after day, phoning and praying brought the same answers: no—no—no; that is, until I turned to the Internet. It was there Assured Assistant Living was presented as reputable, staffed with RNs, and concerned about the elderly. Only six patients were allowed in each of the houses and each was in different neighborhoods that were well-kept both on the exterior and the interior. There just happened to be seven such homes in the Denver area. The price was a different story, for sure. Like my brother had told me previously, "if the money ran out she would come home with me." He was right. I would bring her home with me. With this in mind, the cost did not matter—Mom did.

One phone call to Assured Assisted Living produced the positives I had been praying for. The call was made on a dark evening while pulling into a Safeway parking lot. The owner, Sherry, an RN, picked up. After hearing my need, she told me that the first action would be to evaluate. I prayed that Mom would be accepted, knowing that the nursing home was worsening her condition daily. I kept praying until an answer came. It was the best news I'd had since the trap of rehabilitation directed by the doctor had been meted out.

Rescued

"After seeing and evaluating your mom, we are sure we can help her. All that has happened to her both through surgery and through the neglect she has been receiving can be reversed. Our cost is $4,400 a month. The first and last month's rent need to be paid up front also." Sherry said.

"No problem," I quickly and joyously responded. "I will write you a check tonight if need be."

"That is not necessary. Just bring her tomorrow to 166 Plaid Avenue off of Lincoln and Parker," she said. "We have one bed left in this home. She is only allowed five sets of clothes, a couple of personal pictures, and her Bible. She will also need a walker and wheelchair."

Inside, my heart felt victory over those who were abusing her. "You can't abuse my mom anymore. No more! Never again!"

Protocol would have had me wait until signing release forms and collecting pills before moving her from one institution to another. However, my aggravation spurred me to do whatever I needed to gather up Mom and move her out on my own terms. I took her out of the nursing home not even waiting for the nurses there to get her pills ready, or to help me get Mom in the car. I had cleaned out her belongings, gotten her in the car, and was ready to leave when a nurse came running out to the car. "Here. You will need her Percocet." Laughing, I told Mom, "I could sell these on the streets and get us very rich. But, then I wouldn't want to do that to anyone. Would you?" She only stared out the window with a smile on her face.

As I parked on the neighborhood street outside the Assisted Living Home, Mom seemed as excited as I was. She slid off the seat before

I could go around and help her and held on to the door while my brother got her wheelchair out. It was another one of those stunning autumn days. Mom, now eight-three, kept smiling. Maybe she, too, sensed her new freedom. The air was crisp and clean. Both of us breathed a little lighter.

Soon, my brother would wheel her into the home while I walked by her side. Together, we began putting her precious pictures on the chest of drawers, and carefully placing her Bible on her bed stand. We took her on a tour showing her the back porch, the dining room table, the living room, the dog, and the fish tank, and introducing her to the other residents.

After settling the financial needs with Sheri, it was time to leave for my own home. I had a long drive ahead of me. Mom knew I needed to go. She tried to wave me over to her chair even as I turned to leave. Her eyes were so filled with sadness as she raised and lowered herself in the recliner she was placed into. Her look appeared as a child yearning for attention. I carried that longing look with me as I turned and walked out--sometimes I still see it and pick it up to carry it even though it pains me to do so.

Because Mom was limited in what she could bring in, this meant that we needed to get rid of all of the furnishings and belonging left in the Senior Home where she had fallen. Each day we left her things there, it cost us more and more. She wouldn't be returning; that was certain. My prayer was that at least she soon would be walking in the Assisted Living Home.

More Sizing Down

Getting rid of the smaller things was work but doable. Some things were put into our van; other things were tossed into the dumpster out back. Still other items were given to her friends there. Getting rid of the bedroom set and couch was not as easy.

I asked my brother, "Don't you have a pickup?"

"No," he replied.

"How about your son or a friend?" I continued.

"No. Sorry." He said.

Once again, I prayed and began to phone every listing I could find in the Yellow Pages that offered to take furniture. The major problem was that most of the places wouldn't take used mattresses. I prayed more.

"Would you be willing to take a bedroom set," I said on that last call.

"Yes, we would. Will it cost us anything?" he inquired.

"No, I just need to give it away." I gave him our address and waited.

It had taken me two hours of constant calls when I at last I found someone to take her furniture. I was so delighted when he and a friend came and took everything we had away from the Senior Home. The look on my brother's face was one of surprise, and I wondered why.

The remaining possessions were taken to my home and stored.

Focus on Mom

What we had to do now was to make sure Mom got better. There were only six others living in the assisted living home along with a cute little Pomeranian dog, a large fish tank filled with many colorful fish, and a bird. Each resident had their own leather recliner and remote. The kitchen prepared home cooked meals for every meal, and everyone was bathed or showered each day. The television was mounted to the wall, and surround sound filled the house with relaxing music. It was beautiful, and the change, I prayed, would surely help heal her.

What a difference to see her have a shower every day. This was a special place--a miracle—an answer to prayer. I had prayed for the Lord to help me get Mom out of that nursing home before she died in filth, and He did. Here, she had a clean bedroom with pictures of my father, her beloved husband, and her children. The photos were in plain sight, and believe it or not, a phone was right beside her bed. Her dining table, unlike the spread out zombie like atmosphere in the previous place, was at a table that looked over a green lawn dotted with flowered edges. The little dog ran about her feet, and attendants cleaned every spill.

Her own brown leather La-Z-Boy came equipped with a fur comforter that was specifically hers. If she got cold, she was quickly covered with it. I remember seeing her all white and fluffy in that blanket. Her hair was as white as the blanket, and for a moment, she looked like an angelic being.

On that first day there, when she needed to use the bathroom, the attendant and I helped her out of her wheelchair and walk to the toilet.

She looked behind her before being seated and said, "There are men out there. Be careful and shut the door."

The next day, a young woman came with a guitar and sang to the people living there. She sang songs from the 40's and 50's. When she began to sing this one particular song, it was obvious that the words were complicated and the song long. My mother, the one with Alzheimer's sung every word and never missed a beat. Every one stopped what they were doing and stared at her. When the song ended, she smiled and laid her head back. I couldn't believe what I heard that day.

Hospice

God was "working all of this together for her good" even when Sherri phoned to tell me that my mother needed hospice care.

"Why?" I asked.

"She isn't walking as easily, and her eating has diminished more than I want it to." She answered.

"Okay," I said.

"Don't worry. She still could live a long time. We just need the extra care." She said.

Legacy Hospice would phone me every day. Their care for Mom was wonderful, and their communication skills helped me understand each stage she was entering. Instead of coming once a week, I began to come every other day. It was when my brother had gone on his annual hunting trip, it happened. Hospice had spoken to me about Mom's death. "It might be sooner than we thought," they said.

I couldn't get in touch with my brother. My two sisters were phoned and told the news.

Our Last Visit

Bridget and her son flew out to see Mom. "I'll pick you up," I said mainly because I wanted to rekindle our sister love. I wanted my efforts to overshadow any ideas about law suits and money. "I know that Sam is gone and his wife won't take you to Mom's new place." "Okay," she said knowing that I was right about our sister-in-law, and she hung up.

As I drove down the lane that led to my brother's condo that morning, I saw the silhouette of her back. She was facing the wrong way.

I honked, and she turned. "Get in," I said and smiled. There was a definite distance between us. She didn't smile back. She was facing the wrong way in more than a physical direction. It was as if her mind was removed from the love we had known. Our conversation was plastic. There were no tears as we drove to Mom's beautiful new home.

When we arrived at the home, Mom was sitting at the table with the five other residents. It was breakfast time. Mom had so much food in front of her, more than I'd ever seen for one person. But, she just sat there. We came close. Bridget kept touching her and kissing her. I felt numb. "Mommy." I said feeling odd at the word that left my mouth. Her eyes were closed most of the time. Yellow globs of dried spit filled the corners of her lips. She wasn't drinking or eating. Suddenly, she ate two spoons full of oatmeal then put the spoon down never to touch another thing.

"Can we take her outside for a walk?" I asked the attendant.

"That would be so good for her. Be sure and put her coat on." He said.

We struggled to get her non-compliable arms into the sleeves. She sat in her wheel chair, and we combed her hair. Together, we took her out into the sunlight marveling at the colors and beauty. She spoke, "You two are enjoying this."

"Yes, Mom. We are." I said wondering what she really meant.

"It is so gorgeous. Don't you love it Mom."

She didn't answer.

As we came back around to the home, I bent down to sing Amazing Grace to her when she broke into my melody, "I have to go to the bathroom."

We hurried back into the house. She was taken to the bathroom and scolded for wetting herself. After being cleaned, we took her back to her leather chair and covered her. Out of the corner of my eye I noticed a card from an old friend of Mom's, Anna. It hadn't been opened, and I wondered why.

Mom loved Anna so much. It seemed that nothing on this earth held any importance to her anymore – only moments away and she would leave it all. She struggled to get up from her chair as my sister and I spoke to the RN about how much longer Mom might live. When I saw her struggling, I reached out to help her and soon my sister was trying to help too. She made it just a few steps and fell into another leather recliner. It seemed her efforts had merely built up to fade away quickly.

The next day, Hospice phoned and told me that her passing would be soon, very soon. Would I like to come down? "No," I said. I have regretted that choice ever since.

In The Real Home

'Your Mom has passed. She didn't suffer. And, she looked beautiful in a pink robe lying on her bed." I was told. I gasped and questioned within my heart why. Why had she included the color mom wore. I felt lost, alone, and helpless only to talk myself out of tears because there was work to be done. "A pink robe—beautiful" I kept thinking as I held back the tears.

"Thanks for your kindness. Thank you for all you did staying with her." As I hung up the phone, my efforts at holding back the flood of tears gave way. I knew now she was in the best home any of us could ever want. She could walk and think and talk. She was with Jesus. Still, I cried.

Chapter 8

Changed in a Moment

"The god of this world has blinded the minds of the unbelieving so that they might not see the light of the gospel of the glory of Christ, who is the image of God."
~ *II Corinthians 4:4*

The Best Home

Phoning loved ones to let them know Mom was gone proved to be more difficult than I had imagined. Susy couldn't contain her sobbing when I told her; neither could my mother's brother. He kept repeating, "I told her I would be there no matter what. I promised. I told her I would. But, as you know, my wife has Alzheimer's too, and I can't leave Betty."

"I know uncle. I know," I said hopelessly trying to offer condolences. It took everything within me not to break down. Difficult can't explain how it was to hear him cry. I chocked as I told him I needed to go.

Hospice had helped me, prior to Mom's death, to call a mortuary that would take her body. They gave me a name of a recommended provider. The arrangements were made. Upon notice of her death, they did their job and took her from her assisted living home. For Mom, there would be no more staring at food and water, no more confusion, no more wanting to go home. She was now in the best home of all—Heaven.

Before the mortuary came, however, my sister-in-law came. She picked up the last of Mom's earthly possessions, including her wedding ring. Then, she phoned to inform me. She told me that the hospice worker invited her to come in and view Mom, but she had refused. Knowing her, my mind wanted to chuckle with the thought of how her face would have contorted at the offer.

Meeting a Brother

My brother came home from his hunting trip two days later. At that time, we met at MacDonald's to talk over what needed to be done. To say that I felt uncomfortable around him is to say it in simplicity. I sat on the top of a chair. I couldn't sit completely down in front of him. He made me more than nervous. I remember as we were leaving the restaurant, he saw my little white car and oddly asked "Where did you get that?"

"That is my car. Tim's is the green van I usually drive." I answered. He made sounds in his throat at the answer. I couldn't understand the emphasis on my car. What did he care? Driving away, relief filled my mind.

The next time we met, it would be at the mortuary. He drove in a Jeep. I drove my little white car. He looked it over carefully scrutinizing its tires and observing its interior. I couldn't figure out what he was doing. Trying to divert his attention, I asked, "Isn't it time for us to go in and meet with the mortician?"

"Sure," he answered. "I guess so."

Since Mom's wish was to be buried by my father, three states away, we needed to have her cremated, buy a legal document allowing us to carry her remains across states, and pay for the services. As we walked in to the brick building together, my brother said, "Poor Mom." Then he was silent.

"Did he really think that she was going to feel this? She wasn't poor at all," I thought.

The hallway was quiet—too quiet. The door creaked behind us, and we turned to see if anyone else was there. There was no one. The place felt spooky. I imagined one of the dead rising up and scaring us at any moment. What I didn't think of was how much more scary hidden thoughts were. If only I had known what my brother was really thinking.

We were looking for the office, but certainly, we didn't want to open the wrong door. As we saw signs which read "men's restroom," "woman's restroom," we both decided to use them. They were elaborately beautiful. The marble wash basins were held on ornate wooden posts. The floors were also marble. The water facets were high and curved with wide silvery mouths. Morticians seemingly aren't poor.

It wasn't long before we sat in what appeared to be a salesperson's office. A variety of candies filled a bowl placed just so on the desk. My brother took several chocolates before we began picking and choosing what size vase, what material it would be made from, and what color. "Blue would be lovely," the saleslady said. She kept a sad, low tone to all comments as if we needed her to. It was, I thought, part of her job. Her facial expressions also held forth a gloom and doom look. I wondered what she had to be sad about sitting behind this gigantic oak desk. "Your Mom is right down the hallway if you'd like to see her." She continued.

I had been thinking about Heaven and where my Mom really was now as she spoke. Then it hit me that she had it all wrong. "No she isn't. That is not my mother. My mother is in Heaven. That is just the remains of a life well lived down there. I wouldn't like to see it." I said. "And, by the way, she has medal rods going down her right leg. You might need to know that before the cremation."

"Thank you for telling us that. We will take care of it. And about Heaven and her not being down the hall, true so true," she said. "I just needed to ask if you would like to see her before the cremation," she said.

Then she proceeded with the arrangements warning us that when we got to California they may try to resell us or charge us again for what she was having us pay. She gave us her phone number and said to have them call her if we had any problems.

We were to come back the next day to pick Mom's remains up and take them with us on the eighteen hour trip to the funeral. A date had been previously set with her California church home, and announcements had been sent.

In spite of the joy of going to a celebration of the best new home for Mom ever, there remained to be heaviness in my heart. I thought the worse thoughts about what my siblings were thinking. Sometimes, we let our mind drift into the negative. It is a bad place to be. Because I let it drift, it was a constant battle for me to keep my fears under. As I picked up the urn, it was as heavy as my thoughts. My brother, seeing my grimaced face, quickly said, "don't drop that. It is heavy. You better give it to me." I did as he wished.

Even he had to struggle carrying the urn down the long corridor through the squeaky door and out into the warm air. As we came to our vehicles with the prized possession, he asked, "Do you want to take it to California?"

"I can if you want me to," I answered.

"Well," he began, "I told Mom that I would make sure she got back to her home state. I guess I need to keep my promise."

"No problem," I said. "I will see you at the funeral. Goodbye."

"Bye. I hope this old Jeep makes it," he said with a smirk.

THE LAST GOODBYE

I felt tense saying goodbye to him, and wondered why he was driving that old Jeep for so many years anyway. My brother had made a lot of money during his working career and was retired. His wife was also receiving retirement checks and both also received social security. There was a mistrust that went beyond our childhood experiences as I stood there contemplating our farewell words. I didn't like being around him even though we were related. My parent's had taught us that family is important. Not him though; not him.

Getting over childhood abuses creates a mindset that reminds you to care less if a sibling likes you or not. It was tiring having every word or move scrutinized by this man. I didn't like that either. As I drove away from the brick mortuary with its eerie pretenses, I wondered who this man I called brother was. Being married and living far away from him for forty-seven years creates spaces that allow for different thinking.

Long before Mom had passed away, my husband and I spoke of not living in the seclusion Mom had chosen to in her old age. We would want to be with our children and grandchildren and influence them for Christ's sake as much as we could. We would want to live each day as fully as possible.

Since her death, then, it was decided to sell our big home and travel.

We also had considered all of our "stuff." We didn't want our children to have to get rid of it as we had had to do for Mom's things. We sold our home in less than two weeks after placing it on the market and bought an older RV. In this, we drove out to the funeral.

The excitement of a newly turned leaf in our life mingled together with the responsibilities as we arrived. My pastor husband would preside over the funeral service. Mom would have liked that. She also wanted us to serve those attending lunch. She had spent many hours serving other friends and their family's lunch after funerals in her church and had told me that this was what she wanted as well – to bless others. We would park in my Mom's old driveway, now owned by my daughter.

We could visit with her and my sister, Bridget, who was already parked there permanently. I had brought many personal items Mom had crocheted, sewn, or had held on to for years to lie out on a table depicting some of the life she had lived. Later, these would go home to the siblings who wanted them. When I was taking them out of the back of my car, Bridget saw some shelves I had put in there. She asked for them. "Those are mine," I said. "We are moving, and I thought I might need them."

"Oh," she replied. There was no embarrassment for asking, at least not for Bridget.

There was food to buy and arrangements with the church to be made. I would need their kitchen and some help understanding it. The ladies there were absolutely a blessing. They even offered to help serve. The morning before the funeral I spent cooking and decorating.

There were around fifty folks who came to show Mom respect at her passing. Many stayed to eat the broccoli casserole, fruit salad, cake, and pasta salad or to sip on tea or coffee. Many simply gave out courage and support. The rushing around and fixing for the funeral left me drained and in need of the love they gave. Many spoke of the deeds Mom had done for them or the kindness she had shown. Others hugged me and told me they loved me. Bridget and Susy and some of the grandchildren were mulling over her things and taking what they wanted. My brother had walked outside and was pacing up and down. He had a look of utter hatred and disgust at this whole funeral. More than anything, I was glad it was over, and I could go home and begin to live my life again without all of this responsibility.

Upon the First Day of the Week

The next day was Sunday. I couldn't wait to go to the church that had so kindly helped us and show them my appreciation. The pastor's message blessed me, though for the life of me I can't remember what he preached on. I do remember that he came up to me and my daughter and shook our hands and spoke words of kindness to us. That meant a lot.

After the service, I decided to take my daughter to the same Chinese Restaurant my parents had gone to for years. While we were there, both of our phones began to beep signaling messages coming in. Then, they began to ring off the hook. When we sought to answer them, there was a click. The messages were violent and filled with cursings. "Get your blankity blankity blank over to the meeting right now. You are a blankity, blankity liar." One from Bridget's messages read "Sam and I r at suzies U need to come over for that meeting." In another she wrote, "If u had done what u said u were going to none of this would b happening! Why should I believe you when u lie?" She hadn't even taken the time to spell her words.

In my decision to go to church, I had thought that my siblings would understand. They didn't. Sunday, to them, was just another day. Taking my daughter out to lunch provoked them even more. Even Bridget, who lived at my daughters, when asked to come with us said, "I hate those gossipy Baptists." At the time she said that, I didn't really understand why in the world she would say such a thing. The people at Mom's church had done nothing but bless us.

After eating faster and driving back to my daughters to take her home, I needed to find my youngest sibling's apartment. I had never been there. The directions my daughter gave me were a little unclear causing me to have to turn around and go over the roads looking for the turn off two times. At last, I found the turn off and was outside Susy's apartment. I did not know the right apartment and tried to call my brother, who did not answer, Bridget, who also did not answer, and then tried to knock on any door and ask, when finally Susy came out to escort me into what would become the greatest nightmare I'd ever experience.

As we climbed the stairs to her apartment, I said to her, "this is evil. I can feel that this is extremely evil." "No it isn't," she said. "They just want to talk to you." We continued our climb in silence until at last I stood in the doorway of her very cluttered apartment. Her husband was a hoarder, so there was just a tiny passageway revealing my brother and Bridget sitting. Soon Susy took her place beside them leaving me standing in the doorway alone.

My brother rose and pointed his finger at me, his arms extended he said with a violent tone: "Sit down. You sit down. I said sit down. You better sit down." It was then that his arms began to flail the air. His face got redder and redder as he continued. He looked so silly and somewhere in the depths of my soul, I wanted to laugh. His next sentence sobered me right up. "Mom and Dad are dead." Why had he said such an obvious sentence? Of course they were. We just finished having Mom's funeral. He didn't stop there, though. "I've hated you all of my life. I am going to take you to court and see to it that you are put in jail," he continued.

What in the world was going on, I thought. At some point in the ravings, I could see Bridget sitting there stiff and smiling never once looking at me. In my heart that day standing there, God urged me not to give an answer or even speak. There were times in the past that I hadn't listened to God. But, I was listening now. I turned and walked out. When I got into my car, I burst into tears.

Chapter 9

Relinquish Your Rights

*Revenge... is like a rolling stone,
which, when a man hath forced up a hill,
will return upon him with a greater violence,
and break those bones whose sinews gave it motion.*

~ Albert Schweitzer

BROKEN

The tears couldn't be contained as I drove into my daughter's drive way and ran for our RV. Sobs came uncontrollably. Even within the arms of my husband, comfort was nonexistent. Prayer brought only helplessness and hopelessness to my heart. I still wasn't fully trusting. "How could I? God had let this happen hadn't He. Why?"

There is a childhood saying that tells us that "sticks and stones may break our bones, but words will never hurt." The words that had been hurled at me by my siblings had hurt more than imaginable. When Bridget drove into the driveway, I went to her RV, my face stained with tears and streaked red. "Mom's lawyer wants to see me." I told her. Bridget said, "I want to go too." "I don't think you can." I continued. "She asked to see the trustee only." When I said this, she turned her back on me raising again those fearful feelings of mine. This was a fight I never wanted and didn't know how to stop.

"What do you want? Do you want my portion of the inheritance?

You can have it all? What is it that you want? Oh, Bridget. Stop it." I cried. She merely looked at me as if discussed. I broke down in wails and ran, once again, to my RV to hide the overflow of tears. It seemed they would never stop. From my hiding place, I heard her engine start. She was pulling out of the driveway.

I asked my daughter, "Where is she going?"

"She is headed to her daughter's apartment in Reno. She won't be back as long as you are here." She answered.

"What had happened to our love for one another?" I silently questioned.

I wanted to be rid of this job and the fear it brought. I wanted not to feel helpless and hopeless any more. I wanted my family back. I was brought to attention by the ringing of my phone. The paralegal on the other end was asking me to bring all of my paperwork in as soon as possible. "Could I bring them tomorrow?" I inquired. "Yes, that would work for us," she said.

Lawyer Number One

I soon shifted from trying to patch things up between my sister and I and began, instead, the search and gather process. The task took me the rest of the day—day after day. As I dug through the piles of papers sorting and organizing, I had no time to mourn. I wanted to sob and never get out of bed again, but there was no time given to the trustee to mourn, even though there was a loss of siblings and a mother. Inside, I understood that if one is the trustee, there is no honor or rest in the job description. No one allows the trustee to mourn, especially when they believe you have deprived them of what they deserved. There also is no comfort for a trustee against being blamed, hated, or accused.

As I arrived at the destination the next day, I saw that, Mom's lawyer like the mortician, had an office that far exceeded the normal person's pocketbook. It was set against the backdrop of the high Sierra Mountains. The view was beautiful. Old pines stood here and there dropping cones onto the cedar flower beds below. Bottle Brush with its reds touched the corners of the building as one walked up its twisting paths made of brick. The setting was in an old town that had existed during the gold rush days. Broken wagon wheels and parts highlighted the landscaped flower beds here and there as well.

After entering the building, I was seated in a glassed in seating area towards the back of the massive office. There, I looked over the gold panning paintings, and images of squirrels, deer, geese, and elk on the walls. Soon I was awakened from my gazing by the paralegal. "Glad to meet you. I am Ginger. Please bring your paper work and follow me." She said with her hand out to shake mine. I rose and followed.

She sat with me and asked for bank records, house sale notes, the apartment purchase, and every other record that would reveal how the money came and went. Once she had all the papers, she asked if I could come back again in the morning. She would need to copy all the papers and have the lawyer approve them before she proceeded. What a short visit it was after driving the hour to get there.

The next day, I drove up to the mountain splendored office and waited again in the glassed room. Again, the paralegal called me to follow her. Together, we entered a room decorated in dark cherry wood. The table filled most of the room. The chairs were padded in burgundy and black. The lawyer came in and sat down beside me. The paralegal was across from me. And the papers were spread out before the lawyer. She spoke to the paralegal and me for about thirty minutes. I tried to ask a question once but was quickly told just to listen and do what I was told. She said things will go faster that way and cost less.

It all seemed so odd to me to have to relinquish my rights. I knew that for this short meeting, I would be paying a big bill from the trust money. I had never dealt with such a business as this before. It was a business where the person paying had no rights. When the bill for seeing her came, I realized why she had shortened our conversation. After driving back to my RV home, I fell to my knees beside the bed and cried more. I didn't want to be a trustee. "God help me." I prayed.

Lawyer Number Two

Two months later, I was receiving calls to verify each piece of paper that had been copied that day. In the end, each of Mom's four children was sent the final accounting for her trust. The monies were ready to be distributed. I was shaking inside and crying all of the time now. I thought surely this is what a nervous breakdown feels like. And, then the letter came from my sibling's lawyer.

January 11, 2012

Re: Accounting for the Trust

Dear MS. LASSITER:

This office represents Sam, beneficiary to the Trust, established on July 10, 2001. Demand is hereby made for the entire trust estate to be handed over to him and further demand is made for an accounting for the year 2011. We expect this on or before January 31, 2012. Please feel free to call our office with any questions.

Kindest regards, A Professional Law Corporation

The date the letter arrived to me was January 15th; the accounting he called for needed to be to him before January 31st. How in the world would I do that? Not knowing where to turn in answering such a letter, I phoned my mother's lawyer, the one who had sent out the accounting. "I am not a defense lawyer," she said. "Obviously, we won't be distributing the monies. Instead, we will need to send a copy of the trust to all of the grandchildren who want a copy of it. This is in case the dispute goes on beyond your mother's children's lifetime." She furthered. A letter was sent to all of the grandchildren. I waited the allotted three months to see who would want a copy. Then, while in Washington, I mailed out a copy to each one who requested it.

Mom's lawyer was disappointing. She could not help me fight each thing my sibling's lawyer was throwing at me. I needed to find a defense lawyer. But, how? I spoke to my son, who was a corporate lawyer, and he advised me to let him choose a California lawyer who could actually fight. I let him. And, I cried all the more because I didn't want to fight.

A person gets sick to death when their siblings hate them. That same person's heart fails when they know that their brother and sisters want to put them in jail. I wanted to be counseled and consoled. My husband was unable to give me what I longed for – assurance that all would be okay. My friends wouldn't be able to help me either. It was difficult to find anyone who knew what I was going through. My husband had a golfing buddy who talked to me once over lunch. He had been a banker and had seen many trusts go to court. In the end, he said, all he saw was loss. He said that the trustee could do pretty much whatever they wanted since the responsibility had been given to them. The Lord seemed to be removed from me, but He never was. I just didn't see Him in this. "Where in the world could I find any peace?"

By this time, we were living in Washington state to be with two of our sons. One of those sons was going to be gone for a while and wanted us to stay and take care of their house. My husband was with me for a while but then decided to drive the RV back to Sioux Falls, where another son lived and where his golfing buddy lived. We had put some of the money we got from selling our home into a small farmhouse there. He wanted to do some repairs and unpack. This left me alone for three months in Washington. The grey clouds moved in most of the days. The house was empty except for a couple of cats that scurried about once in a while. And, it was extremely cold as the moisture from the ocean filled the air.

Occasionally I would get a phone call from Mom's lawyer asking me more questions so that she could appropriately answer the questions posed to her by my sibling's lawyer. She would often warn me of the danger I was in, which added more stress. Then, she began to turn my case over to accountants for another accounting. They asked me so many details about the money that sometimes it would take me days to look up that information and get it back to them.

Selling the Apartment

At the same time, I was dealing with the accountant; I was trying to settle the sale on the apartment complex I had bought. The gentleman who decided to buy it at the price I had listed wanted me to loan him back $30,000 that he would be taking out of his 401k. I said that I would do this knowing that if I didn't get the money into the trust account, my siblings would be even angrier. The problem with Gregg was that he was demanding, controlling, and persistent.

I remember him coming over to see the apartment building when I still lived in Cheyenne. "You have painted the entire outside, I see" he said. "Show me the places where you have painted the inside." I had painted the middle apartment and the lower one. The upper apartment, I hadn't. "Are you going to paint this one too?" he asked. "The lady has lived here for five years and is just about to move. I was going to wait until she was out before I started that task." I replied. "Oh, I see." He said. "If I buy the building, will it be painted before the purchase?" he asked. "What if I just buy the paint and leave for you?" I inquired. "I guess that would work," he said. And finally he stopped badgering me over paint.

There had been a hail storm, so the entire roof and some of the decking had to be replaced. The insurance had paid for that. I thought that they had replaced the deck outside the upper level apartment and said so. That deck was a barbecue deck. He corrected me. "I didn't see a new deck on that upper level." He said. I went to check. He was right, so I phoned the roofing company only to be told that the decking under the shingles had been replaced, which was more than ten thousand dollars to have that done. I told the potential buyer about what deck was replaced.

There were shower repairs, stairs replaced, water heaters cleaned, tiles put on the backs of sinks, and windows replaced. All of it had been hard work, for the most part, but Gregg, the buyer, was looking it all over now inspecting and asking as many questions as my sibling's lawyer was. He left that day with all the details I thought any person could possibly want. But, he phoned the next day with more questions. Sometimes he phoned two or three times a day for over two months. When the final papers were signed, I held my breathe praying in desperation for the sale to be done. All of it together was adding more stress to my life than I ever wanted. And, then, I needed to write a check from the trust to give him the second I had promised.

It was while I was in Washington, that I had attended church as usual on Sunday. My husband was not with me that Sunday. As the pastor began to preach, I began to cry. He preached on Philippians 4: 6-9. It was the praying part of my life that wasn't alive--mistrust had overshadowed it. I so needed prayer, for God had been urging me to trust—fully trust--, and I hadn't. "Be anxious for nothing, but in everything by prayer and supplication, with thanksgiving, let your requests be made known to God;" (Phil 4: 6, KJV).

PRAY FOR TRUST TRUSTEE

It is unusual these days for a pastor to give what used to be called an altar call, but this Sunday the pastor did. My tears overflowed unashamedly. It was impossible for me to stand there pretending that all was well in my life. I found myself walking towards the waiting arms of two men who would pray with me.

They asked me what I wanted prayer for, and I told them. Then, they prayed, and I cried more. In my heart, I believed the Holy Spirit was there. My life of mistrust and self-sufficiency was going to change because I was going to change. I was going to listen to God even through the lawyer's threats. I was beginning to learn what He meant when He asked me to trust Him—to fully trust Him.

My daughter-in-law had given me a book for Christmas, and in my depression, I decided not only to pray more, but to read more of what others had gone through. As the pages began to turn, so did my mind. I began to realize why the depression had so overtaken me. It wasn't because my brother hated me, my sister betrayed me, or that my youngest sister joined hands with the others. It wasn't because Mom had died and left this responsibility to me. It was because I was unthankful for what I had.

I had forgotten or never realized that "God is in the details; God is in the moment. God is in all that blurs by in a life---even [our] hurts..." (Voskamp 54). When I went to my knees that day, after reading that God was living and walking right by my side, in spite of the threats that came through the mail, or in special conference meetings with lawyers, or in papers demanded, I focused on God being so near. "Oh, please forgive me, God. How could I have forgotten how much you love me?" I prayed. "Help me. Open up my eyes that I might see "the goodness of the Lord in the land of the living" even this day (Psalm 27, 8).

That day, I stepped outside after prayer and began to see things I had not noticed before. "Mama birds poking worms down their baby's throat on our sidewalk. A puppy chasing and tossing a toy for the first time. Skies full of oranges, pinks, and blues at sunset." How does a person begin to be blinded from all of this beauty? When we think only on the hurts, the wrongs, and the hatreds, that is when the blindness begins. Most people walk through this life blind. I didn't want to be one of them anymore. I wanted to live fully. I wanted to trust.

The law suit wasn't over. It had only really begun. There still would be days when I would be searching for just the right papers. There still was a house that needed to be sold outright. My siblings wanted their money in cash and did not want to have note money sent to them monthly. I would have to walk through this. There was no getting out of it for the trustee. But, praying every day and believing He was alive and with me, was beginning to take away the weakness and sickness that had kept my heart downtrodden.

I would walk through this with my eyes longing and looking for Him first. With Him by my side, I would tackle the challenges. And I would learn to let Him take my fears. When I began to shift my focus on God and all He is doing, when I began to see Him in everything good, I began to lift my head and know that whatever happened, He would be there blessing me with gifts. In fact, He was giving me so many gifts every day that it was hard for me to see them all and thank Him for all of them. He could even give me gifts in jail, just as He had for Paul so long ago, I thought.

Voskamp wrote also that "we do not see the material world for what it is meant to be: as the means to commune with God." (99) When I went to my knees the next day and the next, I thanked Him for full, crimson peonies bursting to bloom-blood red, for cooing doves in the cool of the morning, and for a raccoon sneaking into the tall grasses by the road when our headlights hit him in the face. Then, I would face the day's challenges.

Lawyer Number Three

My new, defense lawyer, urged me to get a loan for my daughter, sign for her, or see that she got one. I would go to the bank here in Washington. I began with Wells Fargo. There I would talk for my daughter, for myself, for God. Actually, I would talk for all of us. As I began to explain to Patty, the financial loan officer there, she sat behind a large desk. She began to cry with me as my story began to take form. Of course, my hands were shaking, and I held my head down. Though I knew that God loved me, I felt shame for being in this situation. I was surprised that she cared enough to empathize with me. "What kind of a woman was this officer," I thought.

She was the God used up miracle kind of woman. That is what she was—a miracle. "How many loan officers cry with you and then work like crazy to make a loan to a girl who had never gotten a loan before happen?" I thought. It took four months before the loan was finished, but in the end, my daughter, got a loan. The house was paid for, and the money was deposited into my lawyer's account for safe keeping.

I felt like a hero, but I wasn't. God was. I knew better than to overlook that. I knew better than to fail not to give Him thanks for this. "God gives gifts, and I give thanks, and I unwrap the gift given: joy." (Voskamp 43). The money was deposited into the trust.

Of course, my siblings were not finished. Still they pursued me. Over the year that had passed, I had learned that I could not, like Job, give God thanks for the good things only. I needed to thank Him for the trails too. "Corn in the fields that grew an inch with last night's rain, for a mother who sacrificed so much to leave this trust money for her children, and farmers scurrying to their fields in the early morning hours." Toil is part of life, so are trials.

Chapter 10

The Discovery

> "Deep in unfathomable mines
> Of never ending skill,
> He treasures up his bright designs,
> And works His sovereign will."
>
> ~William Cowper

DISCOVERY

I never knew what a discovery was. In my mind, discovery was exciting and fun like the childhood game of "button button who's got the button". The legal definition of a discovery is not only confusing but doesn't sound a bit entertaining. The definition is: "A category of procedural devices employed by a party to a civil or criminal action, prior to trial, to require the adverse party to disclose information that is essential for the preparation of the requesting party's case and that the other party alone knows or possesses." (legal-dictionary.thefree-dictionary.com), and I was soon going to understand the rules of a game that wasn't fun at all.

My sibling's lawyer, the one who could not get me to sign over the entire trust to my brother, was now looking for any flaw upon which he could build a case. He had gotten the accounting along with my siblings from Mom's first lawyer, but that didn't satisfy him. No sir. Discovery scrutinizes from every possible angle. The object of the game is money. The fun of the game is to watch the other person squirm.

My siblings wanted satisfaction. They were positive that there had to be more money than what they saw in the first accounting. That thought drove them to pursue at all costs. They had their lawyer demand paperwork showing collected and deposited rent money, proof that I had never lived in the apartment, proof that I had sold the apartment, proof that I had gotten the money for the sale of Mom's old place, proof that I had deposited her car sale money, proof that I had taken Mom to Walmart or out to eat, proof for monies spent for the funeral, and proof about every other thing they could think of where money was involved. Proof, proof, proof, and more proof. They never did ask me how much I paid for from my own money.

The game of discovery hurts because is cuts into the heart of the one being pursued. Imagine a deer. When hunted, there are trees, rocks, and bushes to hide behind. There is protection within the elements that God has created for them. This causes the game of hunting to be fairer. For the hunted human being involved in a discovery, there is no protection apart from the hand of God. Even when God's hand is upon you, the heart is allowed to become contrite and broken. The wounds from each insulting investigation deepen. When the next round comes, lawyers begin to pour salt into them by uncovering whatever they believe touches the pursued person most. Healing those wounds never completely happens. There will always be scars. Over the years, the scars begin to change the person in all three areas of life: the physical, the mental, and the spiritual.

THE ASHES THAT REMAIN

Physically, lighthearted jesting disappears, and either overeating takes place or deprivation or abstaining from foods occur in hopes of soothing the pain. More wrinkles appear on the brow. Sleep is difficult to obtain. Mentally, there begins to be a questioning about oneself. Did I do this or that wrong? Why did I put so much effort into thinking that Mom would live longer than she did? The thoughts about oneself become clouded with disgrace and disappointment. Trusting others becomes even more difficult, and you are somewhat sure that others don't like you anyhow. Spiritually, fear tries to hide

God from you and doesn't allow you to enjoy relationships. The spirit becomes broken like a horse who is broken to the bridle. The spirit simply does what it is told without joy or fun anymore. Sermons heard, prayers given, and songs sung cut deep into all of the parts of your being. The hands meant to rise to God hang down.

It is as if everyone sees you for the sinner you are. "You are ugly, ugly, ugly indeed," you think. At last, you begin to believe all the negatives told you as a child. Every time the phone rings or there is a text message, fear causes anxiety. Surely, it is time for jail. Long ago, I had determined that if I was put in jail, I would preach Jesus to all I came in to contact with. Paul of the Bible had done it. I could too.

Many video games today seek to train the game players to kill, imprison, or destroy. Discovery seeks the same revenge. The game strives to expose the hunted and hide the hunters behind camouflage. When I mentioned to my third lawyer that Bridget's new living quarters were on Mom's old property, the lawyer's justification was "she is paying rent, isn't she". "Yes, she is but only one hundred a month. There is nowhere else one can live and pay that little." I said to no avail. I had forgotten that I was the hunted and had no trees to hide behind. Everything for me, the hunted, had to be out in the open.

When I debated with my lawyer to not pay my brother for carrying Mom's remains to California because I could have done that for nothing, he said, "It is easier just to give him his way than to fight him." "Okay. I guess." I said. The rules of Discovery are not meant to be fair. They are meant to create a winning point for the opposing side.

Discoveries are not only painful physically, mentally, and spiritually, they take time. The first discovery took over a year to process and examine. The lawyer my son had recommended was one of the most expensive and experienced ones in California. "Mom," my son told me, "I recommend Dan because his reviews show that he wins more of these cases than most, and you need the best you can get. You are being sued. Don't forget that." My son did not tell me that it would take years to end this battle. I guess he didn't know. A lawyer never really knows or cares how long the fight will be. They are in the battle for one reason: money.

In the end, the discovery did not prove fruitful. My siblings were unable to uncover any evidence in any of the avenues they sought to prove guilt. A year gave way to yet another discovery to be called for. This next discovery called for the very same papers, so finding the paperwork went a little faster, but writing up the reviews took just as long to finalize. The expenses for each discovery with all of its processes ranged close to ten thousand dollars each time. After all the papers were gathered and sent again, no fault again was found. My lawyer was pressing to take the entire case to court and get it settled.

SEEKING FINALIZATION

Conferences with my son in one city, my California lawyer in another, and me wherever I was at the time, were unnerving. Most of the conversations were between my son and my lawyer since they spoke the same language, and I didn't. Terms such as counsel, beneficiaries, distributions, assertations, objections, settlements, entries of orders, and perjury had to be put into context to understand. I simply wasn't skilled at this without the use of a dictionary.

On one of those conference dates, I was at a friend's home in Phoenix painting with her. She knew that the law suit was going on, so I asked if I might do this in the bathroom for privacy, and she said "sure." It felt so odd to be standing in the bathroom looking at myself in the mirror while the two of them addressed final distribution. Once in a while I would interject. "I will take the note that Gregg had been given," I said. "You will?" my son said. "Good," my lawyer replied.

The two of them went on in conversation with one another and made plans from there while I kept looking in the mirror. "My how old you have grown," I thought placing my fingertips into the creases by my eyes. At last, they finished talking and I listening. Finally, it was time to leave the bathroom. The conference call was ended. It was time to go back to my friends table and resume the painting project I had begun. "All is well," I told my friend. "Thanks for praying."

"Good. I am glad for you." She replied. No more was said about it. We had better things to do.

SEEING

Through all of this, I was growing. I recalled how I had written in my journal about a soaring hawk I had seen whose wings were spread while his eyes were keenly searching the field for mice. Survival meant uses all that God had given him to its fullest. Through practicing trust, my faith was growing stronger. More frequently notations were made of what God was doing on any given day—on any given moment. Those blinded eyes, blinded from the focus on the negatives in life, were seeing the Light more clearly. I thanked Him: "For a strong, faithful husband sleeping beside me; a stately, ring-necked pheasant standing tall in the short corn; and for cows bellowing in fields." What gifts were mine? I prayed that my siblings could see Him too. I was sure He was giving them gifts. I wasn't sure they could see.

Court dates were set. Not being sure if my presence was needed, I called my son to ask him about this. His answer was that only my lawyer and my sibling's lawyer would go before the judge on the appointed date. At this particular court hearing, the honorable judge of the Sacramento Superior Court entered, at long last, Minute Order dismissing the matter.

After the judge's decree, my lawyer had drawn up papers seeking settlement and distribution of the funds and an end to the fight. Sending the papers off first to my sibling's lawyer, all of them signed for the distribution to take effect. However, he had written that the distribution should be to three of the beneficiaries, which excluded me. I didn't sign. This caused the battle to continue for another four or five months.

When at last the court date was set and the judge saw the mess that had been going on for so long, he asked about my sister, Susy. "Are her disabilities mental," he asked my lawyer. "I do not think so," he answered wrongfully. The Judge hit the gavel, and said, "This needs to end. Get the papers signed by June." And he walked out. I continued to trust and pray that this would end. The most important thing in my life now was to trust—fully trust. For, to fully trust, is to fully live as God would have us. Trust is a life lived abundantly.

Chapter 11

Distribution

"God created the world out of nothing, and as long as we are nothing, He can make something out of us."

~ Martin Luther

OPEN YOUR EYES

Abundant life calls for us to open our eyes to the reality that God is in all things and over all things. Too often, we walk about as if this is not true. Too often, we miss Him in our days. When a morning awakens us with the chirping of birds and the rays of light, He is there. With all of the joy that the Lord would have us to know, even while He knows the prince of this fallen world bids us to find flaws, this great God, our Lord and Savior, longs for us to see. Through all of this earthly world and its universes, He is declaring His love and asking us if we see. He is asking if we hear Him as well.

Jesus said, "He who has ears let him hear." Not only does God want us to see the truth of His love all around us, He wants us to hear it. Listen to the laughter of your grandchildren, the sounds of animals all about, the sounds of wind beneath a cloud's gentle breezes as it moves the darkness away to reveal light.

This day, He was asking me to open my blind eyes and see the papers signed, sent through the mail, sitting on my table, the papers that were releasing me from a four year long law suit. "It is I," He spoke to my heart. "It is I who has sustained you through all of this. It is I who loves you beyond your wildest dreams. It is I. Do you see me in the papers?" I ran my fingers over my siblings signatures and tried to remember when we had loved one another. I tried to love them and touch them as I traced the letters before me, but I couldn't.

Seeing Him in the papers before me, tears of delight ran down my cheeks. That morning, I spoke to God with my hands raised. I said aloud, "I see You. I hear You. Won't You help me never to forget this seeing and hearing? What a great and mighty God you are. Help me to share You with all who will see You in sweet, sweet watermelon, in flowers by church doors, in grandchildren hugging , and in lady bugs.

Open human eyes God that they might see. I know now that so many, like me, are walking through their lives as if they merely want an escape from Hell or to have a socially acceptable life on earth. Lord, I know now that what You want is to freely give to Your created loved ones that abundant life You told us about in Your Word." I vowed that day to see and hear of Him every moment He gave me and to continue to write down the blessings I saw and heard. I vowed to share, too, the love He had so freely given me with those I came in contact with.

Informal Accounting

Along with the gift of the signed releases, came a call for informal accounting. The informal accounting would reveal whatever money was left for distributing. Sitting before paperwork that, by now, was perfectly organized, I wrote down what assets were left, where they were kept, and what my fee as trustee would be. Within that accounting, my brother would be given the eight hundred dollars for carrying Mom's remains across the borders and to the funeral home. I would be given the promissory note Greg had signed during the sale of the apartment and would receive monthly payments for that. The other siblings would be given cash for the sale of the apartment, cash for the sale of Mom's house, and cash for whatever was left in the account.

After my lawyer received my informal accounting, it was determined that I had shortchanged myself, and they added on to that amount two more years pay. I was utterly dumbfounded that I should receive anything let alone an increase to that pay. I opened my eyes to this news and knew that God was in this too. How could I not clearly see Him by now? He was working in every fine detail.

Perhaps the finest detail of all had to do with my sister, Susy. Within my mother's will, I had been appointed to be Susy's trustee. Because of her disability, Mom had thought she needed special care over her inheritance. Mom had also been concerned about her husband getting his hands on the funds. He had abused Susy, forced her to cash her disability checks, and had spent them every month for the twenty years they had been married. In the signing of the release forms, Susy had asked their lawyer to include a special exception for her. She had asked that our brother be her Trustee. She wouldn't fully release me unless I signed over that authority to him.

My lawyer son was the first to find out about this. He phoned me. "Mom," he laughed. "This is the best part of the entire closing. You won't have to be responsible for her. And, you won't have to put up with her husband. In my mind, you are truly released." In my mind, however, I saw God again. Perceiving that He was in this, I signed her request and sent that in to the lawyer as well. He loved me. He always had. That night there were flickering lights of fireflies dancing around our front yard, and I saw Him again.

Chapter 12

The Lesson of Relationships

"If you love someone, set them free. If they come back they're yours; if they don't they never were."

~ Richard Bach

THE WORK CONTINUES

God has blessed me with children, grandchildren, and a great grandchild. Spending time with them is what, in our older age, we feel is most important. Our RV gives us the opportunity to do just that. When we visit our daughter, the one that bought Mom's place, Bridget leaves. God is still working on me.

My heart is softening towards her. Knowing that she is alone, without the husband she divorced and homeless, continues to remind me of my own blessedness. When the realization comes to me that she has left because of hatred for me, I have to remember that only hatred for our sin comes from God. Hatred for people comes from the Evil One himself. He did not make me to hold hatred in my heart.

One day, God will give opportunity to make amends. For now, there is much more to see of Him and much repairing to take place in my mind, body, and spirit. I continue to pray for my brother to be saved, for he truly must be lonely without God. I long to see Susy set free from her disability. That freedom might not come until she steps into the real life that exists beyond earth, the place where our mother and father already are.

When the meeting had taken place at Susy's home, before the law suit began, she had phoned the next day and had asked for forgiveness. I had been broken by her efforts and told her that without a doubt I would gladly forgive. My love for her remains intact without the scars the others have inflicted. Her name never existed on my sibling's lawyers forms either. She had never truly taken part in all that happened. Even her request to release me as trustee of her funds was only seen by me and the lawyers as manipulation by Bridget and Sam.

The Scars Continue

There were other scars to be had as I continued on living after the four long years of being sued. One Christmas, I was with my daughter. This gave me opportunity to give a Christmas card to my cousin who lived just down the road from her place. My cousin's husband came to the door when I knocked and told me to take a seat. She will be out in a moment. So, I sat.

When my cousin finally arrived, she began to repeat all that was said to me at that meeting long ago: "We are going to put you in jail. We hate you and always have," she said. Then she began to add on information. She said my grandmother would be ashamed of me and what I had done just wasn't in the family picture and that I didn't deserve any money. As I turned to walk back out to my car, she said, "I suppose that your brother's wife was influential in this whole thing. You know that she is sue happy." I just kept walking deflated and upset. I haven't seen or heard from any of my cousins since that time.

Relationships are Difficult

Human relationships are the most difficult inclusions in our lives. I call them inclusions because from birth we have to have them or we die. Mothers, fathers, sisters, brothers, cousins, aunts, uncles, and grandparents all can either cause us joy or grief. If we focus on human beings for our worth, appreciation, love, purpose, and all other quests to fulfill life as it continues along, we will undoubtedly uncover loss, pain, and hurt.

This isn't God's plan, however, that we experience negativity through relationships. He wants, instead, for us to see and hear Him all about us every day; He wants to be our "audience of One." He wants to be our all. When we get ready to leave this place we mistakenly call "home," we will step into the real world where relationships will flourish because they are not tainted with sin. Until that time, He asks us to trust Him.

Perhaps before eternity reveals itself to me, I can reach out to my siblings. At present, they feel no remorse or need to be forgiven, so I will continue to ask God, the One who reveals Himself every day to soften their hearts and save them. Being in the mental state Mom had been in might have given her the ability to forget hurts or maybe not. I can't forget yet. I want to, but I can't.

If, by any chance, you experience a loved one with Alzheimer's, are appointed as trustee, and are sued in the end, I pray that in some way my story will encourage you to look, as I am still looking, at His presence in all the gifts He gives so freely every day.

www.ingramcontent.com/pod-product-compliance
Lightning Source LLC
Chambersburg PA
CBHW012107090526
44592CB00019B/2676